MW01042951

Espionage and Treason

CRIME, JUSTICE, AND PUNISHMENT

Espionage and Treason

John Ziff

Austin Sarat, GENERAL EDITOR

CHELSEA HOUSE PUBLISHERS
Philadelphia

Frontis: *An expert in spy devices points out the tiny lens of a surveillance system that looks like an ordinary car antenna.*

Cover Photos Top left: NASA; top right: Corbis-Bettmann; bottom right: Corbis; bottom left; PhotoDisc # DT03100; center: Corbis/Bettmann-UPI
Back cover: PhotoDisc # DT03089, DT03093

Chelsea House Publishers

Editor in Chief Stephen Reginald
Managing Editor James D. Gallagher
Production Manager Pamela Loos
Art Director Sara Davis
Director of Photography Judy L. Hasday
Senior Production Editor LeeAnne Gelletly

Staff for ESPIONAGE AND TREASON

Senior Editor James D. Gallagher
Associate Art Director/Designer Takeshi Takahashi
Picture Researcher Patricia Burns
Cover Illustrator Takeshi Takahashi

First Printing

1 3 5 7 9 8 6 4 2

The Chelsea House World Wide Web address is
http://www.chelseahouse.com

Library of Congress Cataloging-in-Publication Data

Ziff, John.
Espionage and treason / John Ziff
    p. cm. — (Crime, justice, and punishment)
Includes bibliographical references and index.
Summary: Recounts the stories of some of the world's most famous spies and traitors, including Benedict Arnold, Aldrich Ames, the Rosenbergs, and Kim Philby.

ISBN 0-7910-4263-4 (hc)

1. Espionage—History—20th century Juvenile literature.
2. Treason—History—20th century Juvenile literature. 3. Spies Juvenile literature. [1. Espionage—History. 2. Treason—History. 3. Spies.] I. Title. II. Series.
UB270.5Z54 1999
327.12—dc21   99–23363
                                                    CIP

Contents

CRIME, JUSTICE, AND PUNISHMENT

Fears and Fascinations:

An Introduction to
Crime, Justice, and Punishment

By Austin Sarat

We live with crime and images of crime all around us. Crime evokes in most of us a deep aversion, a feeling of profound vulnerability, but it also evokes an equally deep fascination. Today, in major American cities the fear of crime is a major fact of life, some would say a disproportionate response to the realities of crime. Yet the fear of crime is real, palpable in the quickened steps and furtive glances of people walking down darkened streets. At the same time, we eagerly follow crime stories on television and in movies. We watch with a "who done it" curiosity, eager to see the illicit deed done, the investigation undertaken, the miscreant brought to justice and given his just deserts. On the streets the presence of crime is a reminder of our own vulnerability and the precariousness of our taken-for-granted rights and freedoms. On television and in the movies the crime story gives us a chance to probe our own darker motives, to ask "Is there a criminal within?" as well as to feel the collective satisfaction of seeing justice done.

Fear and fascination, these two poles of our engagement with crime, are, of course, only part of the story. Crime is, after all, a major social and legal problem, not just an issue of our individual psychology. Politicians today use our fear of, and fascination with, crime for political advantage. How we respond to crime, as well as to the political uses of the crime issue, tells us a lot about who we are as a people as well as what we value and what we tolerate. Is our response compassionate or severe? Do we seek to understand or to punish, to enact an angry vengeance or to rehabilitate and welcome the criminal back into our midst? The CRIME, JUSTICE, AND PUNISHMENT series is designed to explore these themes, to ask why we are fearful and fascinated, to probe the meanings and motivations of crimes and criminals and of our responses to them, and, finally, to ask what we can learn about ourselves and the society in which we live by examining our responses to crime.

Crime is always a challenge to the prevailing normative order and a test of the values and commitments of law-abiding people. It is sometimes a Raskolnikov-like act of defiance, an assertion of the unwillingness of some to live according to the rules of conduct laid out by organized society. In this sense, crime marks the limits of the law and reminds us of law's all-too-regular failures. Yet sometimes there is more desperation than defiance in criminal acts; sometimes they signal a deep pathology or need in the criminal. To confront crime is thus also to come face-to-face with the reality of social difference, of class privilege and extreme deprivation, of race and racism, of children neglected, abandoned, or abused whose response is to enact on others what they have experienced themselves. And occasionally crime, or what is labeled a criminal act, represents a call for justice, an appeal to a higher moral order against the inadequacies of existing law.

Figuring out the meaning of crime and the motivations of criminals and whether crime arises from defiance, desperation, or the appeal for justice is never an easy task. The motivations and meanings of crime are as varied as are the persons who engage in criminal conduct. They are as mysterious as any of the mysteries of the human soul. Yet the desire to know the secrets of crime and the criminal is a strong one, for in that knowledge may lie one step on the road to protection, if not an assurance of one's own personal safety. Nonetheless, as strong as that desire may be, there is no available technology that can allow us to know the whys of crime with much confidence, let alone a scientific certainty. We can, however, capture something about crime by studying the defiance, desperation, and quest for justice that may be associated with it. Books in the CRIME, JUSTICE, AND PUNISHMENT series will take up that challenge. They tell stories of crime and criminals, some famous, most not, some glamorous and exciting, most mundane and commonplace.

This series will, in addition, take a sober look at American criminal justice, at the procedures through which we investigate crimes and identify criminals, at the institutions in which innocence or guilt is determined. In these procedures and institutions we confront the thrill of the chase as well as the challenge of protecting the rights of those who defy our laws. It is through the efficiency and dedication of law enforcement that we might capture the criminal; it is in the rare instances of their corruption or brutality that we feel perhaps our deepest betrayal. Police, prosecutors, defense lawyers, judges, and jurors administer criminal justice and in their daily actions give substance to the guarantees of the Bill of Rights. What is an adversarial system of justice? How does it work? Why do we have it? Books in the CRIME, JUSTICE, AND PUNISHMENT series will examine the thrill of the chase as we seek to capture the criminal. They will also reveal the drama and majesty of the criminal trial as well as the day-to-day reality of a criminal justice system in which trials are the exception and negotiated pleas of guilty are the rule.

When the trial is over or the plea has been entered, when we have separated the innocent from the guilty, the moment of punishment has arrived. The injunction to punish the guilty, to respond to pain inflicted by inflicting pain, is as old as civilization itself. "An eye for an eye and a tooth for a tooth" is a biblical reminder that punishment must measure pain for pain. But our response to the criminal must be better than and different from the crime itself. The biblical admonition, along with the constitutional prohibition of "cruel and unusual punishment," signals that we seek to punish justly and to be just not only in the determination of who can and should be punished, but in how we punish as well. But neither reminder tells us what to do with the wrongdoer. Do we rape the rapist, or burn the home of the arsonist? Surely justice and decency say no. But, if not, then how can and should we punish? In a world in which punishment is neither identical to the crime nor an automatic response to it, choices must be made and we must make them. Books in the CRIME, JUSTICE, AND PUNISHMENT series will examine those choices and the practices, and politics, of punishment. How do we punish and why do we punish as we do? What can we learn about the rationality and appropriateness of today's responses to crime by examining our past and its responses? What works? Is there, and can there be, a just measure of pain?

CRIME, JUSTICE, AND PUNISHMENT brings together books on some of the great themes of human social life. The books in this series capture our fear and fascination with crime and examine our responses to it. They remind us of the deadly seriousness of these subjects. They bring together themes in law, literature, and popular culture to challenge us to think again, to think anew, about subjects that go to the heart of who we are and how we can and will live together.

*　*　*　*　*

Espionage and treason are special crimes in that they are direct assaults on the state. While most crime is treated as an offense against public order, these crimes are directed against the particular government in power or some of its most closely guarded secrets. While most crime does some measurable damage to a particular person, these crimes threaten all of us. Spying and disloyalty to one's country are, for most citizens, almost inconceivable. So powerful is the pull of patriotic sentiment that those acts seem "worse than murder."

To understand espionage and treason we have to look carefully at their history, at the occasions on which they occur, and the motivations of their perpetrators. Some acts of disloyalty are motivated by desperation and by a desire for money. But some are acts of moral commitment carried out in the name of a particular vision of the good. Is it possible espionage and treason are honorable, rather than simply subversive, acts? We need also to attend to the various methods and techniques that spies and traitors use to understand the bravery/foolishness, the daring/ingenuity of their perpetrators.

Espionage and Treason provides a comprehensive treatment of the nature of those crimes. It provides wonderful case studies of actual spies and traitors and a complex examination of their psychology. It asks how we should evaluate the seriousness of what they do as well as gives a detailed analysis of the techniques spies use. This book opens up a critical area of inquiry about all governments, but especially democratic governments: namely, what is the place of secrecy in the rule of law? How much secrecy can any government afford? This book will make fascinating reading for those interested in understanding a truly special category of crime.

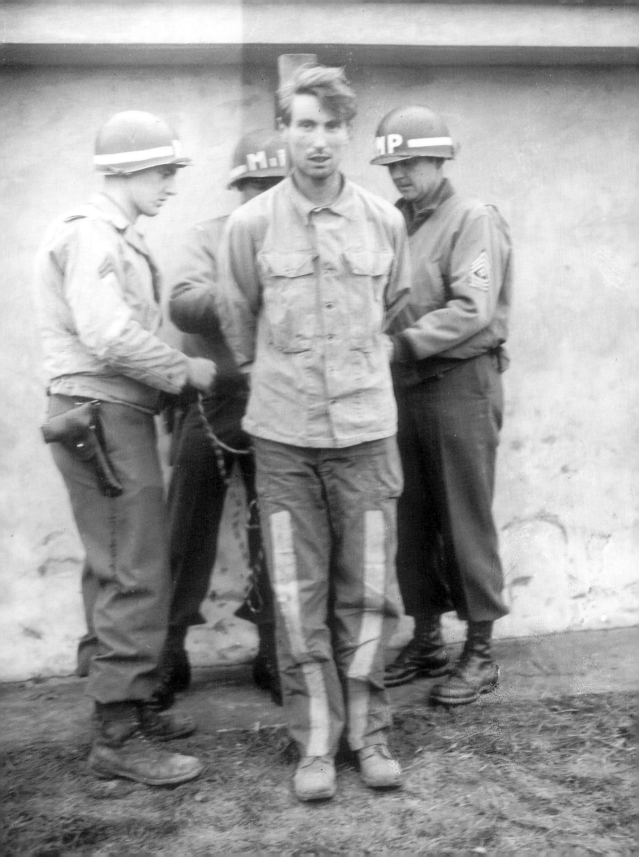

THE DEADLY GAME

In the early summer of 1985, the two most powerful men in the world were sizing each other up like prizefighters before a championship bout. Ronald Reagan, president of the United States, and Mikhail Gorbachev, general secretary of the Soviet Union's Communist Party Central Committee, had yet to meet face-to-face. However, 40 years of icy, often bitter relations between the superpower nations they led, along with a recent escalation of tensions, pointed to difficult times ahead.

Reagan, in the first year of his second term, had taken a hard line against communism and the Soviet Union. His so-called Reagan doctrine called for the United States to oppose the spread of Marxism by arming anticommunist forces throughout the developing world. In June of 1985 one such group was fighting the Soviet army itself. The Soviets had invaded Afghanistan, their neighbor to the southwest, in an effort to prop up the Communist regime that had seized

A German spy is prepared for a firing squad—a common fate of spies during wartime.

power there. Devout Afghan Muslims called mujahedin had quickly taken up arms against the invaders, and the United States had decided to train and supply them. After six years of bloody fighting, the Soviet forces had failed to suppress the mujahedin, and Russian casualties were mounting. The conflict had begun to look like a quagmire from which the USSR couldn't escape.

But in June 1985, Afghanistan wasn't the only problem Mikhail Gorbachev faced. Gorbachev had ascended to the top Soviet post just three months earlier, and he still had to consolidate his power base in the Communist Party, easing out rivals who might oppose his policies. In the long term, Gorbachev planned political reforms and a restructuring of the inefficient Soviet economy. But he realized that the success or failure of those plans would hinge in part on what America did. Reagan had initiated the largest peacetime military buildup in American history, a buildup that targeted the USSR. Economic reform could not occur if the smaller Soviet economy had to match America's massive military spending.

As Reagan and Gorbachev took the measure of each other against the high-stakes background of superpower relations in June 1985, an American and a Russian met for lunch at Chadwick's, a popular Georgetown restaurant only 15 minutes by car from the Langley, Virginia, headquarters of the Central Intelligence Agency (CIA). The men were bit players in the larger drama being acted out by Reagan and Gorbachev and their respective governments. Their business was information.

Over lunch and drinks, the Russian, Sergei Chuvakhin, discussed arms-control issues with his companion, who called himself Rick Wells but whose real name was Aldrich Hazen Ames. The actual reason the men had gotten together had nothing to do with exchanging opinions on ballistic missiles and nuclear warheads, however. The actual reason was to transfer the plastic bags Ames had brought with him. When that occurred Ames officially became, in espionage terms, a Soviet asset. Not only that, he was the rarest and most valuable of all assets: a mole, an agent working inside another country's intelligence organization. Aldrich Ames, who had decided to sell his services to the Soviet Union, was head of the CIA's Soviet counterintelligence branch.

♠   ♠   ♠

"Knowledge is power," wrote the English philosopher Francis Bacon in 1597. In the realm of international relations, Bacon's words ring particularly true. Knowing another country's goals, intentions, or capabilities can provide decision makers with a tremendous strategic advantage, just as being able to listen in on an opponent's huddle would give a football team a huge edge. The need for reliable information about another country and its leaders is most obvious during wartime, when decisions made in ignorance often have disastrous consequences on the battlefield. But even in the more ordinary areas of international affairs—trade negotiations, for example—inside information can give one side a decisive advantage.

Espionage—the practice of spying on adversaries or potential adversaries—is indispensable in developing the kind of information that leaders need to make wise choices. It is not the only source of information they need. In fact, the raw data unearthed by spies is often not immediately usable. It must be compared to information from other sources, analyzed, and then interpreted. The ultimate product, called intelligence, serves as a guide in charting a foreign-policy course.

The use of espionage dates to ancient times. In the Bible's Book of Joshua, which describes events from the 13th century B.C., the Hebrew leader Joshua dispatches two spies to the city of Jericho in advance of the intended Hebrew conquest of the region. In 510 B.C., the Chinese general Sun Tzu wrote a textbook of military tactics that described, with great foresight, the importance of spies. In *The Art of War*, Sun Tzu commented, "It will not do for the army to act without knowing the opponent's condition, and to know the opponent's condition is impossible without espionage." Sun Tzu's ideas about espionage have withstood the test of time. He recognized the power of bribery in turning enemy spies to the other side. He also saw that deception could be a powerful tool, and he achieved deception in a particularly ruthless fashion: He sent some of his spies into enemy territory with information that, unbeknownst to them, was false. Then he deliberately betrayed them. Under torture they would reveal the false information he wanted his enemy to believe.

In the modern world, espionage has become even more critical than it was during the time of Joshua or Sun Tzu. Warfare has become much more destructive, and weapons are infinitely more lethal. A devastating attack can come with little or no warning. The danger is not limited to foreign countries; terrorist groups can inflict serious damage as well. In addition, the sheer quantity of sensitive information and sophisticated technologies that can affect a nation's security is astounding. A country that fails to protect its secrets or that is caught unaware of a threat can pay a huge price.

Yet if spying is essential to a nation's security—and on occasion, to its very survival—espionage remains a morally ambiguous enterprise, especially for a democratic society such as the United States. The values we cherish include openness, truthfulness, and privacy. In the espionage business, secrecy, lies, and deception are the operating principles; human frailties are exposed and exploited; and rightness or wrongness is very much a matter of one's perspective.

Espionage is also a peculiar crime. Virtually all governments spy on other governments, often by recruiting (and generously rewarding) citizens of a targeted

Spying is an ancient practice, as reflected in this illustration of a biblical story in which a woman living in the city of Jericho hides two Hebrew spies. The men had been sent by Joshua to scout the city's defenses, prior to an attack by the Hebrews.

nation to gather and pass on secret information. Yet all governments treat espionage committed by their own citizens as a serious crime subject to substantial penalties.

Espionage in the modern world can be seen as a kind of high-stakes game, with unwritten rules governing the conduct of—and protecting—certain players. Everyone knows, for example, that embassy staffs harbor a number of intelligence officers whose real job, spying, is masked by a phony "cover" position. Counter-intelligence services try to discover the identity of these officers and thwart their activities. But if the intelligence officers employed at their nation's embassy are ever caught engaging in espionage—an illegal activity—diplomatic immunity protects them from any punishment more severe than expulsion from the host country. Of course, when one spy operating under diplomatic cover is expelled, another will soon be dispatched to take his or her place, and the never-ending game continues.

♠   ♠   ♠

The plastic bags that Aldrich Ames handed to Sergei Chuvakhin at Chadwick's contained a variety of sensitive documents, including communications between CIA headquarters in Langley and various stations around the world. More important, the bags contained a list of names. The 11 people on the list constituted virtually the entire roster of top Soviet intelligence officers the CIA had managed to recruit to spy for the United States. They were members of the Soviet State Security Committee, or KGB (the Soviet counterpart of the CIA), and of the Chief Intelligence Directorate, or GRU (the USSR's military intelligence service). In the weeks following the lunch at Chadwick's, the flow of information coming to the CIA from these sources dried up. At the same time he allowed the Soviets to see inside America's intelligence establishment, Ames in effect blinded his own country to the USSR's intentions.

For the men on Ames's list, the consequences would be severe. No nation looks kindly on traitors, and the Soviet Union took a particularly dim view. Most of the men were shot. A KGB training film—no doubt intended as a warning to others who might spy for the United States—showed one man being lowered alive into a blast furnace.

As a 23-year veteran of the CIA, Ames knew what would happen to the men he betrayed. But if the

Aldrich Ames, a high-ranking CIA official, enjoyed making a little extra cash on the side—as a spy for the Soviet Union. The USSR paid Ames $2.7 million for information between 1985 and 1994.

unhappy ends they met ever bothered him, he never showed it. He appears to have considered it all just part of the deadly game of espionage. In his mind they had assumed the risk when they got into the game in the first place, and in particular when they decided to spy for the enemy—even though that enemy was Ames's own country.

For his part, Ames had decided to work for the Soviets because he needed money. A divorce had cost him dearly, and his girlfriend Rosario (who later

became his wife) was unaccustomed to living frugally. In April 1985 he had walked into the Soviet embassy in Washington, D.C., and handed over an envelope containing some low-level intelligence, suggesting that he be paid $50,000 for his efforts. The Soviets complied. Ames later claimed to have conceived the transaction as a scam against the Soviets—he'd extract some money from them for marginal information, then be done with the whole business. But of course the promise of more money got him hooked. After the meeting at Chadwick's, when the Soviets realized the incredible value of what he had provided—and thought about how useful he might be in the future—they informed Ames that they had set aside $2 million for him. Financially, things had started to look up for Aldrich Ames.

The Central Intelligence Agency overlooked several clues to the identity of its "mole," Aldrich Ames, including his cash purchase of a home in Virginia (opposite page). Information provided to the CIA by a Soviet defector, Vitaly Yurchenko (at left), helped to divert suspicion from Ames.

Tradecraft—the procedures to be followed for success in espionage—dictated that the KGB not immediately move against the Soviet spies Ames had fingered. Doing so might tip off American intelligence analysts to the presence of a mole. Tradecraft dictated that an asset as valuable as Ames, who might come along once in a lifetime, not be exposed to possible detection. Despite this, the Soviets hastily rounded up the traitors in their intelligence services. But Ames, through a combination of good luck and CIA short-comings, remained undetected for years, outlasting not only the presidencies of Ronald Reagan and Mikhail Gorbachev but also the Soviet Union itself.

Ames's good luck may have stemmed in large part from a coincidence. On August 1, 1985, right around the time the Soviets were moving against the agents that Ames's information had exposed, a KGB official named Vitaly Yurchenko defected in Rome. When he first heard the news, Ames must have sensed disaster. As a colonel, Yurchenko was senior enough to have been briefed about the KGB's mole inside the CIA. No doubt Ames's dread increased when he was assigned to meet Yurchenko at Andrews Air Force Base in Washington the next day, and thereafter to play a leading role in debriefing the Russian. Unbeknownst to Ames, however, Yurchenko had been transferred from the KGB's counterintelligence section in March 1985 and thus knew nothing of the KGB's high-placed mole. What he did know—and what he told his American debriefers— was that a former CIA officer, code-named ROBERT, had divulged information about American espionage efforts against the USSR. Although Yurchenko never knew ROBERT's real name, he had learned that the former CIA officer had been dismissed right before a scheduled assignment in Moscow. That information could only describe a man named Edward Lee Howard, whom the Federal Bureau of Investigation (FBI) immediately put under surveillance but who managed to slip away and defect to the Soviet Union. The CIA came to believe, for a while at least, that it was Howard who had compromised its best Soviet assets.

But this stroke of good fortune alone does not explain how Aldrich Ames continued to go undetected, even as more CIA operations inexplicably failed and the Soviets arrested more American assets. Much of the responsibility rests with the CIA itself. From 1985 on, Ames lived well beyond his apparent means. He and his wife, Rosario, drove expensive new Jaguars. They bought a house in Arlington, Virginia, for $540,000— and paid cash. They bought an oceanfront estate and two other properties in Colombia, Rosario's native country. That they should not have been able to afford all these things on a CIA salary of approximately $60,000 seems obvious in retrospect. But Ames explained away the discrepancy by alluding to a friend who, he said, periodically gave him hot investment tips or by claiming that the money came from Rosario's family in Colombia (who were actually of very modest means). The real explanation, of course, is that the Ameses' lavish lifestyle came courtesy of the USSR. Over the course of his espionage career, the KGB—and the intelligence agency that replaced it after the fall of the Soviet Union—funneled some $2.7 million to Aldrich Ames.

But other things besides Ames's obvious wealth should have raised red flags at the CIA. He had a serious drinking problem, and he was often drunk in public. Supervisors caught him failing to report all his contacts with Soviet officials, as CIA rules required. He even showed signs of deception on CIA-administered lie-detector tests. Somehow he managed to convince the examiners that his emotional stress had an innocent explanation, and when they gave him follow-up exams, he passed.

For nearly 11 years, Aldrich Ames sold some of America's most sensitive intelligence secrets to the Russians. Sometimes he met with his Soviet handlers in foreign cities, such as Vienna, Austria, and Bogotá, Colombia. Other times, he left secret information in dead drops (containers concealed in out-of-the-way locations) in the Washington, D.C., area. In return the Soviets lavished money on him. They even set aside a beautiful tract of land along a river in Russia, where they would build the man they called their "dear friend" a *dacha*, or country estate, when he was ready to retire. And why not? In the high-stakes game of espionage, the Russians were scoring big against their American adversaries—and their superstar player was the well-connected traitor at the CIA.

"Worse than Murder"

The Constitution of the United States mentions only four crimes by name. Of these, it defines just one: treason.

"Treason against the United States," Article 3, Section 3 begins, "shall consist only in levying War against them, or in adhering to their Enemies, giving them Aid and Comfort."

As reflected by its prominence in the Constitution, treason has traditionally been viewed as the most serious crime a citizen can commit against the state. In basic terms, treason means betraying the allegiance owed to one's government. Aldrich Ames gave a succinct definition when he characterized his espionage activities as "a switching of loyalties."

But over the centuries, different societies have held differing views about how much loyalty citizens owe their government and its rulers, and therefore about what constitutes treason. The ancient Romans considered any action that jeopardized the security of the

For many people, money has been the motivation to betray their country's secrets by providing information to the enemy.

25

The definition of treason was limited during the rule of England's King Edward III (1327–77). The Statute of Edward III, issued by Parliament in 1351, listed seven offenses considered treason against the crown. They were "compassing or imagining" the death of the king, queen, or heir; violating the king's wife, daughter, or daughter-in-law; levying war against the king; supporting or aiding the king's enemies; counterfeiting the king's seal; counterfeiting the king's money; and slaying the chancellor, treasurer, or the king's justices.

state to be treasonous. This might include inciting rebellion, betraying a Roman army, or assassinating an emperor (though in the latter stages of the Roman Empire, assassination became the customary method of transferring power, and the killers of emperors remained beyond the reach of the law). The convicted Roman traitor could look forward to execution, sometimes after a period of torture. However, the Romans took steps to prevent accusation of treason from becoming a tool of political intimidation. Under the law, a suspected traitor had to be accused in writing, had to receive a speedy trial, and could not be convicted unless he or she confessed or unless multiple witnesses testified against him or her.

Medieval England, on the other hand, saw a proliferation of treason charges. Judges had virtually unlimited power in deciding which acts were treasonous. Because it could only increase royal authority—and because convicted traitors forfeited their property to the crown—kings preferred that the judges err on the side of a more liberal interpretation. Charges of "constructive treason" were common. In these cases, the defendant's actions might not amount to actual treason, but the judge could interpret the pattern of behavior as treasonous. All manner of conduct could—and did—form the basis of constructive treason.

In 1351 the English Parliament finally tried to limit the arbitrary use of treason charges. The Statute of Edward III defined high treason as any of seven offenses against the crown, all of them punishable by death. These included counterfeiting money, giving aid to the crown's enemies, and levying war against or plotting to kill the sovereign. They also included an offense that today seems unfathomably bizarre: imagining the death of the king, queen, or heir to the throne. In the 15th century, a luckless innkeeper paid with his life for this offense. Walter Walker had tried to placate his misbehaving young son by telling him that he would make him heir to the crown if the boy settled down. Although Walker was referring to his tavern, called The Sign of the Crown, authorities interpreted this comment as imagining the death of the king, and the innkeeper was duly convicted and executed.

By this time the intent of Edward III's Statute of Treasons—to limit constructive treasons—had been circumvented. A clause in the Statute of Treasons gave the king and Parliament the power to decide whether an act not listed in the statute was treasonous. Monarchs and ministers seized upon, and often abused, this loophole. The reign of Henry VIII (1509–47), in particular, witnessed some of England's most outrageous treason offenses. These included, according to the English jurist Sir William Blackstone, "stealing cattle by Welshmen; . . . execrations against the King; calling him opprobrious names by public writing; . . . refusing to abjure the Pope; deflowering, or marrying without the royal licence, any of the King's children, sisters, aunts, nephews, or nieces; . . . judging or believing (manifested by any overt act) the King to have been lawfully married to Anne of Cleve; . . . [and] impugning his supremacy." This last charge, especially, represented a fearsome weapon for intimidating opponents and quashing dissent.

Two centuries later, residents of the American colonies were keenly aware and deeply resentful of the British government's power to level constructive treason charges against them. When the Declaration of Independence condemns King George III "For transporting us beyond Seas to be tried for pretended offences," the offenses it is referring to are constructive treasons. Yet at the same time, the Continental Congress had urged the colonies to adopt legislation punishing adherence to the king as treason, and nine of them had complied. Thus, during the Revolutionary War, a person could be threatened with treason under colonial law for supporting the king, and under British law for supporting the colonies.

After the war, America's leaders recognized the abuses that treason charges had produced throughout history. "Most [legal] codes," Thomas Jefferson wrote, "extend their definitions of treason to acts not really against one's country. They do not distinguish between acts against the government, and acts against the oppressions of the government; the latter are virtues; yet they have furnished more victims to the executioner than the former; because real treasons are rare; oppressions frequent. The unsuccessful strugglers against tyranny, have been the chief martyrs of treason laws in all countries."

The men who gathered in Philadelphia in 1787 to draft a constitution for the United States, observers have noted, feared the political use of treason charges more than they feared actual treason. No doubt the Founding Fathers' attitudes stemmed in large part from their wartime experiences. Virtually every one of them could have been found guilty under the British law of constructive treasons. And as they saw it, their only offense had been to oppose tyranny. With that in mind, the Founding Fathers made it difficult for the new American government to bring treason charges against one of its citizens. Not only did the framers of the Constitution borrow every safeguard known at that time to Western law, but they also created two new

Treason can be a matter of perspective: American colonists who opposed England's rule, such as these men pulling down a statue of King George III, considered themselves patriots who were fighting tyranny. However, in the view of English Loyalists, the colonists were traitors.

The men who framed the Constitution of the United States were careful both to define treason and to present clear guidelines for the prosecution of treason cases.

ones. The first was the prohibition against creating new treason offenses, either by judges or legislators. Only what was specified in the Constitution—levying war against the United States or adhering to its enemies, giving them aid and comfort—could be grounds for treason charges. The second built on two protections other societies had developed: the requirement of an overt act and the requirement of a confession or multiple witnesses against the accused traitor. "No Person shall be convicted of Treason," the framers of the U.S. Constitution wrote, "unless on the Testimony of two

Witnesses to the same overt Act, or on Confession in open Court." Whereas elsewhere a treason case could be brought with the testimony of two people who witnessed two separate acts, or with the testimony of one person who witnessed an act and another who discerned a disloyal attitude, in the United States, multiple witnesses had to testify about the same act. This, the framers felt, would lessen the risk of false testimony.

Following the definition found in Article 3, Section 3 of the Constitution, the United States Criminal Code limits treason to instances in which a person "owing allegiance to the United States, levies war against them or adheres to their enemies, giving them aid and comfort within the United States or elsewhere." In large measure because of this narrow definition of the crime, treason charges in the United States have been relatively rare, and before World War II, the federal government had never executed anyone for treason. A few treason cases have involved the levying of war. The Whiskey Rebellion, a 1794 uprising of farmers in western Pennsylvania who objected to an excise tax on whiskey, led to several treason convictions. Treason charges were also brought against a few Confederate leaders during the Civil War. Most famous was Jefferson Davis, president of the Confederate States of America, who was indicted for treason but never tried.

A greater number of treason charges have been filed for adhering to America's enemies, giving them aid and comfort. This offense has two components. Adherence to the enemy, the more subjective of the two, refers to a state of mind—specifically, treasonable intent. Unless a person is motivated by a desire to further the enemy's cause, he or she cannot be guilty of treason, even if his or her actions actually help the enemy. Giving aid and comfort, on the other hand, refers to specific, observable acts. Without such acts, harboring sympathies for the enemy does not constitute treason. But just where mere intellectual or emotional support of the enemy's cause ends and giving aid and comfort begins is subject to some interpretation. The American poet Ezra Pound was charged with treason for making pro-Fascist radio broadcasts from Italy during World War II. Pound never faced trial, however, because he was judged to be insane. Other American citizens who broadcast wartime propaganda from enemy countries, such as the infamous "Tokyo Rose," were tried for treason and convicted.

World War II, probably because it involved not just armies and navies but all sectors of society, led to a spate of treason cases involving the giving of aid and comfort to the enemy. A German-American named Max Stephan, for example, received a death sentence for sheltering an escaped German prisoner of war in Detroit. Another naturalized citizen named Hans Max Haupt was sentenced to life imprisonment for sheltering and buying a car for his son, Herbert Haupt. The younger Haupt was one of eight spies and saboteurs a German submarine landed along the coast of Florida on June 17, 1942. He made his way to Chicago, where his family had lived since the early 1920s. His mission was to get a job at, and later sabotage, an optics plant that manufactured a bomb sight for American airplanes. He never got a chance to carry out that mission, however. Herbert Haupt was arrested less than a week after arriving in Chicago, convicted before a military tribunal, and executed. Because Hans Haupt had known about his son's sabotage mission, a jury decided that in helping Herbert, he had committed treason.

Anthony Cramer, another German-born citizen of the United States, was convicted of treason for helping two other saboteurs in Herbert Haupt's group. While Haupt had gone to Chicago, Werner Thiel and Edward John Kerling had proceeded to New York City. There Thiel contacted Cramer, whom he had known for many years. Multiple witnesses testified that Cramer, Thiel, and Kerling met and "engaged long and earnestly in conversation" at a tavern; that Cramer and Thiel later met and talked at a cafeteria; and that Cramer agreed to hold several thousand dollars for Thiel. On the basis of these overt acts, he was convicted of treason. Cramer appealed, however, and the case ended up before the U.S. Supreme Court. In its opinion in *Cramer v. United States*, delivered on April 23, 1945, the Court amplified the Constitution's two-witness requirement. While conceding that overt acts need not *appear* treasonable to form the basis of a treason charge—many treacherous acts, after all, seem innocent on their face—the justices ruled that all acts used to draw inferences of treason must be "sufficient . . . to sustain a finding that the accused actually gave aid and comfort to the enemy." Though multiple witnesses had testified that Cramer met with enemy agents on two occasions, they couldn't say what the men had talked about, or even whether Cramer had paid for their drinks. In the absence of two witnesses testifying that the meetings actually assisted the saboteurs, the Court overturned Cramer's conviction.

The two-witness requirement had figured less subtly in a famous early treason case involving Aaron Burr, the former vice president. Sometime around 1805, Burr and a former senator named Jonathan Dayton began hatching a plan to carve out a vast empire in the South and West. To this day, the specifics of the plan aren't known for certain; Burr himself told different versions of the events throughout his life. But in appealing to the British minister for financial aid for his plan, Burr had claimed that his intent was to conquer Mexico and separate from the Union all U.S. territory west of the Appalachian Mountains.

In early 1807, with preparations under way for the invasion of Mexico, General James Wilkinson, the governor of the Louisiana Territory, exposed Burr's plan. Burr faced charges of treason at a trial presided over by John Marshall, chief justice of the United

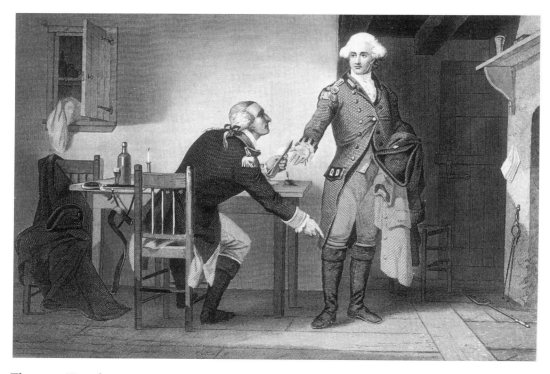

The name "Benedict Arnold" has become synonymous with "treason." In this illustration Arnold suggests to British major John André that he carry secret papers, related to Arnold's plot to surrender the American fort at West Point to the English, in his boot. After Major André was captured and the plot was discovered, Arnold escaped and fought for England.

States. In the end, the former vice president was saved from a treason conviction, and a possible death sentence, because General Wilkinson, whom Burr had earlier recruited for his plan, was the only witness to testify against him in court.

Though the case of Aaron Burr riveted the nation's attention, the most famous treason case in American history occurred a generation earlier, in the midst of the Revolutionary War. The principal figure in that case has become so indelibly linked with treason that his name is virtually synonymous with that crime.

Benedict Arnold had been a true hero of the American Revolution. Only days after the war's initial battle at Lexington, Massachusetts, on April 19, 1775, Arnold, a Connecticut militia captain, developed a plan to take Fort Ticonderoga in New York. Along with Ethan Allen, he led the troops that attacked that British stronghold on May 10. A week later he seized

Fort St. John on Lake Champlain.

In the fall of 1775 Arnold led a column of 1,100 American patriots on an arduous journey through Maine and a sliver of southern Canada to the banks of the St. Lawrence River. Arnold's goal of taking the city of Quebec was thwarted after much hardship and suffering, a desperate New Year's Eve attack on the city (during which he was wounded in the knee), and a siege he directed that lasted until May 1776.

And if these exploits weren't enough, Arnold's fighting retreat from Canada may well have saved America's chances for independence. In the fall of 1776 the British planned to invade and occupy New York from the north, isolating and then strangling the New England colonies. Though the English forces were numerically superior to and better equipped than his own weary soldiers, Arnold's constant harassment delayed the British invasion. In the face of the resistance, the British were forced to shelve their invasion plans as winter approached.

But Arnold's public image as a brave and selfless patriot hid another reality: he had a substantial ego, and he seethed with resentment at his commanders'—and his country's—failure to recognize his talents. After the invasion of Canada, Congress had promoted him to the rank of brigadier general. But the next year it overlooked him in promoting five brigadier generals—men he considered bunglers—to the rank of major general. Furious, Arnold toyed with the idea of resigning, but was dissuaded by George Washington himself.

In September 1777, while commanding the Americans' left wing during an engagement at Freeman's Farm, New York, Arnold launched an attack that his commander, General Horatio Gates, hadn't ordered or anticipated. Though Arnold's actions led to an American victory, in Gates's report to Congress the general did not acknowledge his subordinate's key role. Arnold protested vehemently, and Gates responded by dismissing him. Nevertheless, when the British attacked the American camp several weeks later, it was Benedict Arnold who rallied the men, led a charge into the British lines, and broke through. During the action his horse was shot out from under him and Arnold himself was shot once again in the leg.

His reputation rehabilitated, Arnold became Washington's military commander in Philadelphia after the British evacuated the city in 1778. Soon, however, conflict between prominent Philadelphians and the general degenerated into bitter name-calling. Arnold's critics took him to task for what they saw as his high living. His friendships with Loyalists won him no points among Philadelphia patriots either. Most serious, though, were the allegations of corruption and misuse of his position. Among other things, Arnold's critics accused him of protecting the interests of businessmen in exchange for cash payments, having the army close down stores so he could buy out their inventory and resell it at a profit, and ordering soldiers to run personal errands for him.

Although the allegations spurred Arnold to resign his command in Philadelphia, his critics were not mollified. They insisted that their charges be heard at a court-martial, and George Washington reluctantly agreed.

Before the court-martial convened in December 1779, however, Arnold had dispatched a friend to sound out the British. Perhaps, he thought, they might be interested in paying for his services. They were. Arnold began passing military secrets to the enemy.

That treason pales in comparison with what Arnold attempted after the court-martial board found him guilty of misconduct and Washington issued a mild reprimand. By the summer of 1780, Arnold had managed to have himself appointed commander of the strategically important American fort at West Point, New York. In July he wrote a letter to Major John

André, an aide to the British commander in chief. The message declared his willingness to surrender the fort and its garrison. Arnold suggested a payment of £20,000 for his efforts.

André and Arnold met on the night of September 21 to discuss the plans. Unfortunately for them, American sentries detained the disguised Englishman as he attempted to return to British headquarters, and they discovered incriminating papers in his boot. André received the customary punishment for spies during wartime: on October 2 he was hanged. Arnold, however, had gotten word of the Englishman's arrest and had slipped away.

For the remainder of the war, Arnold fought with the British, though he never again played more than a minor role in the outcome. After the English defeat at Yorktown in 1781, he and his family went to London. He'd been paid about £6,500 during the war and subsequently was awarded an annual pension of £225 for his treasonous work.

Though he was clearly a brilliant and resourceful commander, Arnold failed to get a commission in the English army. What's more, he and his wife, Peggy—who had always been a Loyalist—found themselves shunned by British society. Aversion to traitors runs deep.

Spies, on the other hand, enjoy a certain allure, as evidenced by the many popular novels and movies that feature spy heroes. Yet in some respects espionage is merely the flip side of treason. The intelligence service that can't get foreign citizens to betray their countries will have an inadequate intelligence picture. Ultimately the job of the case officer—the intelligence professional who serves as an intermediary between the intelligence agency and the actual agent—boils down to cultivating traitors. And in the murky world of espionage, one person's traitor can be another's hero. Treason, according to espionage authority Ernest Volkman, "has always

To Americans, GRU colonel Oleg Penkovsky was a hero for passing information about the Soviet Union. The Soviets, however, executed Penkovsky for treason in 1963.

been, and remains, very much a question of which side is doing the judging." The cases of Oleg Penkovsky and Julius and Ethel Rosenberg aptly illustrate that point.

The American intelligence community has always regarded Oleg Penkovsky with a respect that approaches reverence. Penkovsky's CIA code name was HERO. A 1992 biography of the GRU colonel bore the title *The Spy Who Saved the World*.

In April 1961 Penkovsky, assigned by the GRU to gather scientific and technical intelligence about the West, began passing Soviet secrets to American and British agents during an official trip to London. His stated motivation was a belief that the USSR wanted to start World War III. Whether resentment of the KGB also played a role is a matter of speculation. Penkovsky apparently felt that his career advancement had been stifled because of suspicion that his father was not devoted to communism.

Penkovsky was the highest-ranking Soviet military officer to spy for the West during the cold war, and the quality of his information reflected his access. For a year and a half, during official trips to London and Paris, and at home in Moscow, he delivered a treasure trove of reports, documents, photos, and personal insights. Technical data about Soviet missiles, both antiaircraft and ballistic nuclear missiles, probably constituted his most valuable information. But he also detailed Soviet nuclear testing, passed along specifications for the most advanced Soviet tank (which in turn shaped the design of the next U.S. tank), and shed much light on the Soviet espionage establishment, identifying more than 300 KGB and GRU agents.

In Moscow, Penkovsky passed material in dead drops and directly through "brush contacts" in public places with Janet Chisolm, the wife of a British intelligence officer under cover at England's embassy. Some authorities believe routine KGB surveillance of the spouses of foreign embassy workers may have alerted the Soviets to Penkovsky's espionage. In any case, on October 12, 1962, the colonel was arrested. After convicting him of treason, the Soviets executed Penkovsky on May 16, 1963.

Penkovsky was praised in the United States, and his spying was called a courageous effort for peace. In comparison, two American citizens, husband and wife Julius and Ethel Rosenberg, were among the most reviled figures of the cold war era. And yet, their apparent motivations for passing atomic secrets to the Soviet Union during World War II were quite similar to Penkovsky's motivations for his treason. The Rosenbergs saw the USSR locked in a life-or-death struggle with an evil enemy, Nazi Germany, and they believed the Soviets needed—and deserved—American technology to defend themselves.

Neither Julius nor Ethel Rosenberg was a professional intelligence officer. For years some people doubted they were even spies. But those doubts seem resolved in the wake of the Soviet Union's collapse, as previously secret documents have been uncovered. For example, the American writer Richard Rhodes, in his acclaimed 1995 book *Dark Sun*, cites documentary evidence from both the United States and the Soviet Union detailing the Rosenbergs' espionage activities. And Pavel Sudoplatov, in his 1994 memoir *Special Tasks*, also implicates the Rosenbergs. As director of a Soviet committee coordinating wartime atomic espionage, Sudoplatov had been in a position to know.

Julius and Ethel Rosenberg were vilified in America after being convicted of giving secrets about the atomic bomb to the USSR. The Rosenbergs were executed in 1953.

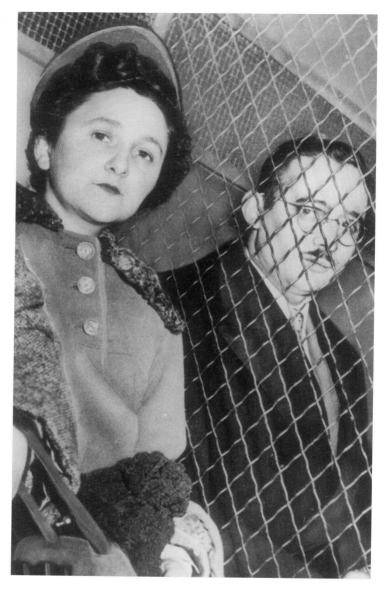

But if the Rosenbergs' atomic espionage has been confirmed, what is also now abundantly clear is that the couple played only a minor role in the massive, and successful, Soviet effort to steal the secrets of the fission, or atomic, bomb. As Sudoplatov points out, "[T]he Rosenbergs were never a significant source.

They were a naive couple overeager to cooperate with us, who provided no valuable secrets." By contrast, the Soviets penetrated major atomic-research centers in England, Canada, and the United States, including the Los Alamos, New Mexico, facility where the first fission bombs were designed and made. They had spies in government, industry, and science. Among their most important espionage assets was a physicist named Klaus Fuchs. The German-born Fuchs, a Jew who had fled from the Nazis in 1933, was a citizen of Great Britain—and an ardent Communist—when he arrived at Los Alamos in August 1944 as a member of the British Mission. His work centered on implosion, one of two methods the scientists were pursuing to create the nuclear chain reaction that would give the atomic bomb its devastating destructive power. In time Fuchs would provide the Soviets with a complete diagram of the Fat Man plutonium-implosion bomb that the United States dropped on Nagasaki, Japan, to end World War II.

Julius Rosenberg, an engineer from New York City, had started recruiting spies from among his former college classmates and passing information to the Soviets by 1942. At the time, the United States and Great Britain were allied with the Soviet Union in the fight against Nazi Germany. Germany's 1941 invasion of the USSR had inflicted horrendous casualties on the Red Army and on Soviet civilians, and for months the USSR teetered on the brink of collapse. In part the country's woes stemmed from its limited industrial capacity and lack of technical expertise in critical areas such as electronics, a cornerstone of modern weapons systems. Apparently because of his Communist convictions along with his revulsion of Nazism, Julius Rosenberg passed information about the American electronics industry to his Soviet control, or handler, in New York. His wife, Ethel, also a Communist, appears to have at least known about her husband's espionage activities. She, like Julius, received gifts and citations from the Soviet Union.

Had it not been for a coincidence, the Rosenbergs would likely have lived out their lives in obscurity. In 1944, however, David Greenglass, Ethel's younger brother, was sent to Los Alamos. An army machinist, he was assigned to make molds for the high-explosive "lenses" that would be used in the plutonium-implosion bomb.

From their many other sources, the Soviets knew that Los Alamos was the center of the atomic-bomb program. Evidently, Julius Rosenberg's control passed this information on to him, because Rosenberg in turn informed his brother-in-law and then recruited him to spy. In New York during a January 1945 furlough, Greenglass gave Rosenberg a sketch of one of the high-explosive lens molds he had machined. He also briefed a Russian contact of Rosenberg's on his work but couldn't answer any of the Russian's technical questions. In June, Greenglass passed more sketches and descriptions of high-explosive lens experiments to an espionage courier in Albuquerque, New Mexico. Some experts have dismissed the value of the machinist's information. But, as Richard Rhodes has pointed out, the common references in the material provided by Greenglass and Klaus Fuchs "would have served . . . as independent confirmation of the authenticity of the information [the] Los Alamos spies were passing."

Thus, through the recruitment of David Greenglass, the Rosenbergs played a role, albeit a minor one, in the transfer of atomic secrets from the United States to the Soviet Union. By all outward appearances, their motives were noble. They wanted to help an embattled country—an ally of their own nation—fend off conquest at the hands of a Nazi regime that, by any measure, was among the most brutal in history. In this respect they resembled Oleg Penkovsky, who sought to prevent the totalitarian regime under which he lived from achieving what he believed to be its goal: world conquest. It should be pointed out, however, that Julius Rosenberg continued his atomic espionage after World War II had ended, persuading Greenglass to write down everything he knew about the bomb in September 1945. In addition, the Rosenbergs always denied that they had ever passed information. So perhaps their ideological devotion to communism represented a larger motivation than their concern for humanity.

Whatever the case, the Rosenbergs weren't regarded as heroes of conscience by the U.S. government, as Penkovsky later was. Of course, by the time the FBI arrested the couple in the summer of 1950, the uneasy wartime alliance between the United States and the Soviet Union had given way to the cold war. The USSR had swallowed up Eastern Europe, and American soldiers were dying in the desperate early weeks of the Korean conflict. Most significantly, though, on August 29 of the previous year, the USSR had successfully tested its own atomic bomb. The United States no longer had a monopoly on the most destructive weapon in history.

The 1951 espionage trial of the Rosenbergs and Julius's friend Morton Sobell took place in a climate of anticommunist hysteria. The presiding judge, Irving Kaufman, summed up the sentiment of many Americans when he characterized the Rosenbergs' crime as "worse than murder" and speculated that "millions [of] innocent people may pay the price of your treason." Kaufman sentenced the Rosenbergs to death. On June 19, 1953, after a series of unsuccessful legal appeals, the couple died within 10 minutes of each other in Sing Sing's electric chair.

OF MICE
AND MEN

For 17 years, until his arrest in 1985, John A. Walker Jr. provided a great amount of sensitive information about U.S. military operations to the Soviet Union. He was well paid for his espionage efforts. Money is one of the primary motivations for treason; others include ideology, being placed in a compromising position, and ego.

"You know," KGB defector Vitaly Yurchenko informed his American debriefers, "if you had gone to war with us during the time of Walker, you would have lost. . . . We would have wiped you out."

The "Walker" Yurchenko was referring to was John Walker, a communications specialist for the U.S. Navy whose time as a spy lasted 17 years—extraordinary longevity in the world of high-level espionage. Whether information he provided would have enabled the Soviets to "wipe out" the United States in a war is a subject of dispute among military experts. At the very least, however, thousands of American servicemen and women, particularly in the navy, would have perished as a direct result of John Walker's treason.

Like the field of espionage itself, motivations for betraying one's country can be complex, multifaceted, and difficult to grasp. For the sake of simplicity, however, espionage experts—and case officers trying to recruit spies—use the acronym MICE to classify the primary reasons for treason. The M stands for money, perhaps the most common motivation among traitors; *I* stands for ideology; *C* for compromise; and *E* for ego.

John Walker definitely fell into the M category. His greed overrode all sense of duty or loyalty to his country. Indeed, it even took precedence over personal ties, for Walker involved not only his best friend but also his brother and his son in a far-flung espionage ring that passed some of America's most sensitive military secrets—all for the purpose of lining his pockets.

In 1964 Walker, a high school dropout, joined the navy to avoid a jail sentence for burglary. Three years later, he found himself in a financial jam. After being assigned as a watch officer to the U.S. Atlantic Fleet submarine command in Norfolk, Virginia, he had sunk his life savings into a bar that he hoped would successfully cater to the many navy personnel in the area. But the bar flopped, and between business losses and the need to support a wife and two small children, Walker didn't have much spare cash to spend on himself, a situation he found intolerable. So on December 23, 1967, the 30-year-old drove to the Soviet embassy in Washington, D.C., asked to see the security manager, and declared his readiness to sell classified U.S. documents. He plopped down a sample: a photocopy of the month's key settings for a navy cryptographic device (a machine used to scramble electronic messages, making them impossible for an enemy to read). Had the Soviets possessed a copy of the machine, the key list would have enabled them to easily decipher submarine messages that month; but because they had no copy, the material Walker provided, though top secret, was hardly of earth-shaking importance in itself. But the Russian security officer—undoubtedly a KGB man—gave Walker an envelope containing about $1,000 and then asked him to sign a receipt for the money. This procedure, standard for the KGB, was designed to make it a little less likely that walk-ins (that is, spies who volunteer their services without being recruited) could end the game on their terms. In the back of their minds would be the nagging worry that the evidence of their treason might surface should they suddenly stop cooperating with their patrons.

Not that the thought of ending his treasonous activities seemed ever to have entered John Walker's mind. On the contrary, he was by all accounts unburdened by guilt and focused entirely on making the money he needed to support a lavish lifestyle.

Soon after his visit to the Soviet embassy, a KGB handler contacted Walker and set up procedures for passing documents—and collecting cash—through a system of dead drops. Any face-to-face meetings would occur in Vienna, Austria; this would make it easier for the KGB to avoid detection. Walker threw himself into his new sideline. Within a year he was earning $4,000 a month from his shadow employer.

Over the course of his military career, Walker received positions of increasing responsibility in the navy—and gained increased access to state-of-the-art cryptographic systems, as well as to the top-secret messages that passed through them. He even volunteered, in 1971, for a tour of duty aboard a communications ship off Vietnam. That assignment not only put him in the midst of technology the Russians coveted but also yielded valuable operational information regarding America's conduct of the Vietnam War. This information included American troop movements and precise times and targets of American bombing raids, which the Soviets passed on to their North Vietnamese allies.

By the mid-1970s, Walker had decided to retire from the navy to enjoy the pleasures of civilian life. But this did not mean that he intended to abandon his lucrative career in espionage. He merely recruited others to spy for him, essentially doing the same thing as a case officer for the CIA or KGB. Walker befriended a navy communications expert named Jerry Whitworth, and after discovering Whitworth's deep-seated sympathy for Israel, he made a so-called false-flag recruitment pitch, lying that he spied for the Israelis. Whitworth signed on. The same pitch worked in the recruitment of Walker's older brother Arthur, a retired navy lieutenant commander who worked for a defense contractor. (A defense contractor is a private company that makes military equipment for the government.) In perhaps his most cynical and reprehensible act, Walker exploited the emotions of a child looking for his father's approval, steering his impressionable son Michael into a career in naval communications and then recruiting him to spy.

Year after year, the Russians fed the Walker spy ring with lavish amounts of money. In return they reaped a bountiful harvest of military secrets, including specifications for U.S. cruise missiles, warship missile-defense systems, spy satellites, and cryptographic systems; the positions of undersea microphones used to monitor the movements of Soviet submarines; American naval plans in the event of a war with the USSR; and even the codes necessary to authenticate a nuclear-missile launch. But Walker's greed, which had motivated his treason in the first place, eventually proved his undoing. In 1984 his ex-wife, miffed that Walker refused to pay the alimony he owed her, reported him to the FBI; she had known about his spying for 15 years. Within six months the FBI had rolled up the most damaging spy ring in U.S. history.

If money is the most common motivator of treason, the second element of the MICE acronym, ideology, has spurred some of history's most single-minded traitors. (Ideology is the body of beliefs and goals of a particular sociopolitical group.) The Rosenbergs and many of the other atomic spies were motivated by an intense ideological commitment. So too were five young men who attended England's Cambridge University during the 1930s. After their university education, the men would rise to positions of prominence in government and intelligence—all the while betraying Great Britain's most sensitive secrets to the Soviet Union.

While a history student at Cambridge University's Trinity College, Harold Adrian Russell Philby, nick-named Kim after the hero of a Rudyard Kipling story, joined the student Marxist organization. He would eventually decide to devote his life to the advancement of communism. Disillusioned with the smug detachment of upper-class English society (of which he was a member) and alarmed at the rise of the Nazis in Germany, Philby, on the eve of his graduation in 1933, asked a Cambridge faculty member and avowed Communist how he could best serve the cause. He was referred to a French Communist group, which then directed him to the banned Austrian Communist Party. At that time, the Austrian Communists were attempting to organize groups in Hungary and Czecho-slovakia. As a courier in Vienna, Philby came to the attention of the Soviets' pre–World War II intelligence service, the NKVD (People's Commissariat for Internal Affairs), which enlisted him to spy upon his return to England. His mission would be to penetrate the British Foreign Office. Philby thus became the charter member of the spy network the Soviets would proudly call the Magnificent Five.

Next to sign up was Donald Maclean, a brilliant linguist who, as an undergraduate, had been a member of the same Communist student group as Philby. Originally Maclean had intended to teach English in the Soviet Union. His handlers, a Hungarian Communist named Theodore Maly and an Austrian Communist named Arnold Deutsch, convinced the idealistic young man in 1934 that he could better serve the USSR—and humanity—by infiltrating Britain's Foreign Office. That way he could keep the Soviet Union apprised of any British plots to subvert the revolution. To do this, his handlers counseled, he should break all ties to

Guy Burgess's belief in communism caused him to betray his country's secrets. While a student at Cambridge University in England during the mid-1930s, Burgess was recruited by fellow students Kim Philby and Donald Maclean to spy for the Soviet Union. Burgess eventually rose to a position of importance in Britain's foreign intelligence service, MI6, and passed many important secrets to the Soviets.

Communist groups in order to avoid suspicion of his politics. Maclean was given the code name HOMER.

On the advice of Kim Philby, Guy Burgess, another Cambridge Communist, was recruited next. He, too, severed his affiliations with Marxist groups and publicly adopted a more conservative political outlook.

Anthony Blunt, the oldest of the Magnificent Five, entered Cambridge in 1926, the recipient of a scholarship in mathematics. He later switched to modern languages and, like the others, became interested in Marxism. While pursuing postgraduate studies at Cambridge, Blunt met Burgess, who persuaded him to work for international communism.

Blunt, in turn, recruited the final member of the Cambridge spy ring, John Cairncross, who entered the university in 1934 to study French and German. He was already a Communist, and Blunt was one of his faculty advisers, which facilitated Cairncross's recruitment.

By the mid-1930s the Soviets had five determined British idealists committed to their cause. As educated members of Britain's upper-class elite, the Magnificent Five could be expected to penetrate the corridors of power. But success did not come immediately. Philby, who had trouble entering government service because of his former, very public espousal of communism, was forced to find work as an editor and journalist. Burgess landed a job as a producer for the British Broadcasting Corporation. Maclean was hired by the Foreign Office but initially had limited access to secret information. Cairncross also penetrated the Foreign Office, but he was moved around too often to learn anything of value.

Throughout these early tribulations, the Magnificent Five's NKVD handlers remained patient. In time their patience would be abundantly rewarded.

Philby went to Spain in 1937 to cover the Spanish civil war, soon becoming official correspondent for *The Times* of London in Nationalist-controlled Spain. From this position, Philby gathered—and passed on to the NKVD—valuable intelligence about the Fascist forces of Generalissimo Francisco Franco, which were opposed by a Republican coalition that included Soviet-supported Communists. Maclean, assigned to the British embassy in Paris in 1938, passed on information about French and British plans to appease Adolf Hitler, which may have figured in Soviet leader Josef Stalin's decision to seek a nonaggression pact with the Germans.

But it was during World War II that the Magnificent Five scored their biggest espionage successes. Blunt got a job in MI5, Britain's counterintelligence agency, where his duties included monitoring governments in exile. Burgess and Philby entered MI6, England's foreign intelligence service. Cairncross worked at Government Communications Headquarters, where he had access to the top-secret decryptions of intercepted German communications. Even without Donald Maclean, the Cambridge traitors would have been of incredible value to the Soviet Union, for between them they penetrated virtually the entire breadth of the British intelligence establishment.

But Maclean was a star among stars. He had become one of the Foreign Office's most well respected and trusted officials, with access to virtually all the diplomatic secrets of the British government. He dutifully shared everything with the Soviets. In 1944 he was sent to Washington, D.C., to assume a position on the Combined Policy Committee, which had been established a year earlier to coordinate work in Great Britain, Canada, and the United States on an atomic

Donald Maclean's wife Melinda, shown here with their three-month-old son shortly after her husband's disappearance, received the telegram on the facing page, in which Maclean explains that he "had to leave unexpectedly." Warned by Kim Philby that he was under suspicion, Maclean fled to the Soviet Union with Guy Burgess.

bomb. In this capacity Maclean betrayed a range of secrets that helped the Soviets gauge the direction of the Allied bomb program.

After World War II, Great Britain and the United States, uneasy allies with the Soviet Union in the fight against Germany, became bitter enemies of the USSR. The cold war was beginning, and the Magnificent Five continued their espionage for the Soviets. Maclean, still in Washington and privy to atomic secrets, revealed that the United States' nuclear arsenal was small. This information enabled Stalin to swallow up Eastern

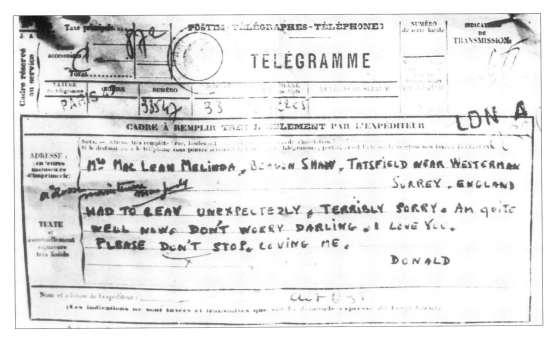

Europe without having to worry about American nuclear retaliation. In 1950 Maclean, now head of the British embassy's American section, passed on another priceless bit of information: that the United States would not use nuclear weapons against, nor would its forces invade, China as a result of the Korean conflict. Lin Pao, commander of the Chinese army in Korea, would later declare that without this knowledge, China would never have entered the fighting in Korea, during which some 52,000 American soldiers ultimately lost their lives.

For his part, Kim Philby steadily climbed the MI6 hierarchy, all the while betraying scores of British espionage operations and exposing numerous spies to the Soviets. By 1950, when he was chief of station in Washington, D.C., serving as liaison to the American intelligence community, it was assumed that Philby would become MI6's next head. That would have been a disaster of unimaginable proportions for Great Britain—and, for that matter, for the United States.

Harold "Kim" Philby jokes with reporters during a 1955 press conference, after being formally cleared of suspicion that he had tipped off Burgess and Maclean. Philby, the first member of the Cambridge Five, had risen to the top of Britain's MI6. However, suspicion that he was the "third man" in the spy ring never went away, and he was eased out of the intelligence organization. In 1963, he defected to the Soviet Union.

But in that year Philby was informed that American intelligence, having recently decrypted Soviet wartime cables, was closing in on an agent code-named HOMER. From an initial group of 600 suspects, the FBI had eliminated all but 6. Maclean was one of them. Philby dispatched MI6 colleague Guy Burgess to warn Maclean, and the two men slipped away to Moscow and defected.

It was readily apparent that another high-placed source, a "third man" in the spy ring, had tipped off Maclean and Burgess. Suspicion quickly fell on Philby, who was eased out of MI6 but never prosecuted, perhaps for lack of evidence or perhaps, as some experts have suggested, to avoid embarrassing the British government or making public more secrets. Philby defected to the Soviet Union in 1963, as another investigation seemed to be closing in on him as the third man. Blunt and Cairncross had by this time ceased their espionage activities, and the existence of a fourth and fifth member of the spy ring wasn't suspected. Eventually, though, the two were publicly exposed (Blunt in 1979, Cairncross in the early 1990s).

If strong personal convictions inspire the treason of ideologically motivated spies such as the Cambridge Five, personal weakness is at the heart of the third major motivation for spying for an enemy: compromise. Intelligence services and the case officers they assign to recruit foreign spies sometimes dig up evidence of illegal conduct or personal indiscretions—or they entrap a potential asset in compromising behavior— and then blackmail the person into doing their bidding. Sexual indiscretions have been a staple of this recruiting technique. The KGB, for example, recruited many agents with the so-called honey trap: a female agent would seduce a married man, and the two would be photographed having sex. If the man didn't agree to spy for the Soviets, the KGB would threaten to send the incriminating photos to his wife. Homosexuality has also been a source of compromise.

But blackmail need not be a requisite for compromise. Agents are sometimes assigned to win the affections of an unmarried person, and the targeted person can then be coerced into spying out of his or her love for the agent. East Germany's spy service, the Ministerium für Staatssicherheit, enjoyed particular success with this technique by targeting lonely, middle-aged women who worked in West German government offices. And sometimes, especially with men, sex alone, in the absence of deception, is sufficient for compromise. During World War II, for example, an American-born British agent named Amy Elizabeth Pack became the lover of Captain Charles Brousse, an official of the Nazi-controlled Vichy government of

France. Pack made no secret of her mission to steal France's diplomatic ciphers. Brousse willingly helped her, and the two later married. Pack also used sex to pry information from a Polish diplomatic aide about the Germans' Enigma enciphering machine, a device used to create messages in an unreadable code.

The final MICE category, ego, embraces those whose high opinion of themselves and their abilities leads them to treason. Benedict Arnold is perhaps the most prominent example of a traitor motivated by his enormous ego. But compromise by ego can be more subtle than going over to the enemy because of the belief that one's talents aren't adequately appreciated or rewarded by one's own country. Some people are led down the road to treason by intellectual flattery. For example, a case officer under cover as an academic or scientific expert might commission a person with technical or diplomatic knowledge to write an article on an unclassified aspect of his or her expertise. Praising the finished article's insightfulness, the case officer will commission further assignments, which will receive similar praise. Eventually the author may be asked to write on a topic that is classified or may simply be asked to pass information to the person who has been commissioning his or her works. As implausible as this recruiting angle sounds, it has been used successfully. For example, in 1947 Soviet agents began recruiting a Canadian academic named Hugh Hambleton in precisely this manner. Between 1956 and 1961, when Hambleton served in the North Atlantic Treaty Organization, he fed NATO secrets to his KGB handlers.

Like all attempts to categorize the motives for complex human behavior, the MICE framework is imperfect. Not every traitor fits neatly into any of the four categories. For example, after the CIA fired Edward Lee Howard for drug abuse and other personal problems, he sold all the information he knew to the USSR, which probably makes his motivation for treason mere revenge. Then, too, one person sometimes has a combination of motives, and it may be difficult to assess the relative importance of each. Jonathan Pollard, a U.S. naval intelligence analyst, had an ideological motive for passing secrets to Israel: he was an enthusiastic Zionist and felt that the United States was withholding intelligence the Israelis needed for their defense. But Pollard also accepted money for his services.

In spite of its shortcomings, the MICE classification does make clear a key point about treason: morally not all traitors are created equal. At one end of the spectrum are traitors such as John Walker and Aldrich Ames, who were willing to trade lives for their own monetary gain. Such people can claim no justification for their mercenary actions. At the other end of the spectrum lie ideologues such as the Cambridge Five and the Rosenbergs. While today it may be hard to understand how intelligent and educated people could have overlooked or rationalized the murderous excesses of Stalinism, these people believed deeply that their actions were moral and right. They saw their disloyalty to their country as loyalty to a higher good—namely, the possibility of a better future for all of humanity.

Somewhere between those who betray for money and those who betray out of adherence to an ideology fall traitors motivated by ego or by compromise. The former have a character flaw, for which they probably bear much responsibility. Nevertheless, their actions are perhaps more understandable—and slightly more excusable—than are those of people motivated solely by greed. The latter, people who have been compromised, also probably have a weakness of character, but they can be viewed more sympathetically. They may, in fact, be more victim than criminal.

Like the world of espionage itself, the world of treason defies moral absolutes.

Jonathan Jay Pollard is an example of a spy with several motivations. Pollard was a U.S. Navy intelligence analyst who provided information to Israel. Pollard's motives were both ideological (he felt that his information was essential to Israel's survival) and monetary (he accepted payment for his activities).

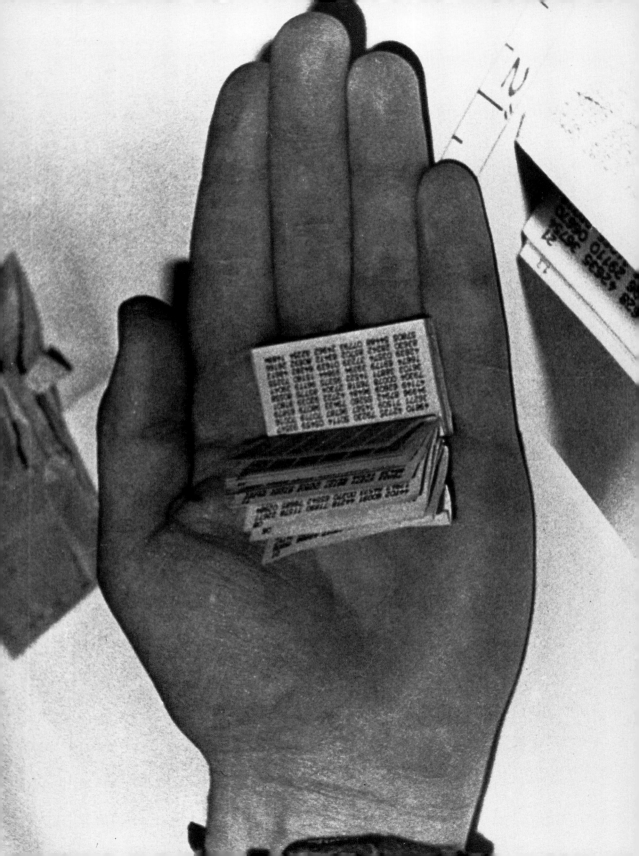

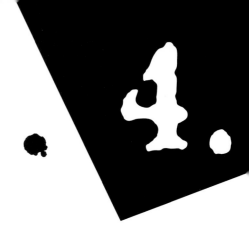

READING THE ENEMY'S MAIL

A s the Americans closed in for the kill, Admiral Isoroku Yamamoto, the architect of Japan's surprise attack on Pearl Harbor, may have marveled at his extreme bad luck. How could a squadron of 18 P-38 Lightning fighters, without benefit of onboard radar, find his aircraft in the vast blue emptiness of the Pacific skies? While the majority of the American fighter planes cut his escort of nine Zero fighters to ribbons, four P-38s peeled away from the main formation to finish off Yamamoto's slow and helpless transport plane.

The killing of Japan's greatest naval officer, which struck a devastating blow to that country's dwindling hopes for victory in World War II, appeared to be the result of a lucky break for the American armed forces. In reality, the April 18, 1943, engagement over the Solomon Islands was anything but a chance encounter. Admiral Chester Nimitz, commander of the U.S. Pacific Fleet, had personally ordered the attack on his

This is a seven-page code pad, containing groups of numbers based on the code words "New Orleans" and "Seaport." Reading an enemy's messages is an important component of espionage.

Japanese counterpart. The American commanders knew Yamamoto would be inspecting Japanese naval bases in the area that day; in fact, they knew his entire itinerary, down to where and when he would be eating lunch. The reason was not because America had a spy in the Japanese military but because, far from the rattling machine guns and exploding bombs, a small group of American mathematicians and linguists had figured out the cipher system Japan used to radio military commands among its far-flung Pacific bases. The United States was, in effect, reading its enemy's mail.

The interception and decoding of secret communications played a major role in World War II, and almost no one would question the appropriateness of these activities during wartime. It's unlikely that many people would find reading a potential adversary's mail during peacetime ethically problematic, either. Reading the mail of an ally during peacetime, however, is considerably more troubling. The fact remains, however, that friends do spy on friends. Notions of fair play and conventional morality that apply in daily life don't govern the activities of intelligence services.

If the goal of espionage is to discover sensitive information, there can be no more reliable source than the targeted party's own words. For this reason, spies have always devoted much effort to intercepting confidential communications, and those trying to thwart spies have devoted equal effort to protecting their communications. As technology has advanced, the methods on both sides have become increasingly complex.

Throughout most of history, writing was the only reliable method of long-distance communication. To keep important messages secret if a letter fell into the wrong hands, generals and rulers saw the need to make them unreadable to all but the intended recipient. The Roman general Julius Caesar used a simple cipher to protect his messages. He replaced each letter in the message (in espionage terms, the actual information the sender wants to be conveyed is called *plaintext*) with the letter that was three places further along in the alphabet. Thus the word *legion* would be written *ohjlrq*. While today such a system could probably be deciphered by a high school student of average ability, the low rate of literacy in the first century B.C. made it secure enough.

The cipher disk, a version of which was invented by the Italian scholar Leon Battista Alberti in the 15th century, operated on the same principle as Caesar's cipher, with an additional wrinkle. The disk consisted of two concentric wheels (or four, to accommodate numbers) upon which were printed the letters of the alphabet. The outer wheel could be rotated, enabling the operator to line up any letter with the inner wheel's *a*. The wheels were then locked in place and the outer wheel used to encipher what was spelled out in plaintext on the inner wheel. The recipient would have an identical cipher disk; to read the message, he or she needed to know the initial position of the outer wheel. Although the cipher disk was considerably more complex than Caesar's unchanging three-letter-forward substitution, it could still be defeated. The reason: the

Codes and Ciphers

Though the terms are often used interchangeably, a code is distinct from a cipher. In a code, the plaintext words the sender wishes to communicate are replaced by letters, words, numbers, or symbols that have arbitrarily been assigned a certain meaning. To use a simple example, a location might be signified by a number (100 = New York; 101 = Dallas; 102 = Seattle), or the word *Tuesday* might mean "Meet at the usual place tomorrow." The key is that both the sender and the receiver have the same codebook.

A cipher system, on the other hand, alters a plaintext message (often with the aid of a mechanical device) through the systematic substitution of numbers or letters for the original letters.

Both systems of concealing the meaning of sensitive communications have been used extensively throughout history, and messages can be both coded and ciphered for extra security.

varying patterns of letter frequency in a given language. In English, for example, the letter *e* appears in 60 percent or more of the words, while the letter *q* is rarely used. A cryptanalyst (someone who solves codes and ciphers) seeing many *p*'s in a disk-enciphered message might begin by assuming *p* equaled *e*. Arab scholars had discovered the principle of cryptanalysis through letter frequency by the 14th century. In the West codebreakers would begin using that principle during the Renaissance, when the establishment of permanent embassies led to an explosion in spying.

In spite of its shortcomings, the cipher disk was still in use at the time of the American Civil War. By then, however, other methods of protecting written communications were also being used. For example, secret writing was done with so-called invisible inks, a time-tested method that had been widely used by Revolutionary War spies. Invisible inks cannot be seen when they dry; they must be made visible. This usually involves applying heat or a chemical reagent to the message. Civil War commanders made use of a relatively new technology as well: telegraphy. The telegraph transmitted messages almost instantaneously, without the use of paper and ink. However, spies could steal a copy of the message at the telegraph office, so sensitive information still had to be encoded or enciphered.

In the years between the Civil War and the first decade of the 20th century, telegraphy became the primary mode of transmitting messages between embassies and their home countries. To ensure secrecy, foreign services developed massive diplomatic codebooks. Relatively little effort went into breaking other nations' diplomatic codes, because few people grasped the potential importance of intercepting and deciphering diplomatic traffic carried through telegraph lines. According to espionage authority Jeffrey Richelson, only three countries—France, Russia, and Austria-Hungary—had centralized cryptanalytic

bureaus before 1914.

World War I would change that. The four-year conflict, which saw the introduction of poison gas, aerial
combat, and tanks, also witnessed the military use of
a more benign technology: radio. Radio revolutionized
cryptology, and even espionage itself.

The transmission of information via radio waves, a
technology pioneered in the 1890s by the Italian inven-
tor Guglielmo Marconi, had been used for ship-to-ship
and ship-to-shore communication. It had also been
used on occasion by news correspondents filing stories.

But with the outbreak of World War I in August

*Telegraph messages had to
be enciphered to keep the
information from falling into
the wrong hands. Equip-
ment such as the Beardslee
telegraph machine was used
during the Civil War to keep
military messages from being
read by the other side.*

1914, radio assumed a vital role in military communication. It enabled headquarters to communicate easily with frontline units, to order rapid troop movements, and to mount highly coordinated attacks along lengthy front lines. And, unlike the telegraph, it required no transmission lines, so radio transceivers could go virtually anywhere. However, because radio was broadcast, anyone, including the enemy, could listen in. For that reason, guarding the security of codes and ciphers became very important.

Not everyone immediately comprehended this new reality. Ill-trained Russian radio operators and cipher clerks in particular cost their nation dearly. Communications security dictated that all messages be enciphered before being transmitted in Morse code. But Russian radio operators often broadcast completely in the open or enciphered only certain important words. Worse, they sometimes broadcast the same routine message openly, and later broadcast an enciphered version. This enabled German cryptanalysts to break Russia's ciphers.

The consequences on the battlefield proved catastrophic. For example, Russia's war plans called for its First and Second Armies to envelop Germany's Eighth Army in Prussia in the first weeks of the war. But the Germans intercepted a series of unenciphered radio messages sent between Russia's two advancing armies. The messages told the Germans all they needed to know about the Russian forces and their objectives. When an unenciphered message revealed that the First Army had halted its advance in order to resupply, the German forces quickly massed near Tannenberg, where the Second Army waited. The Germans launched a massive offensive on August 27, 1914. As the battle raged, they monitored Russian radio transmissions and learned of the Russians' plans for a counteroffensive. By August 31 the Second Army had been routed, with 30,000 Russian soldiers killed and another 90,000 captured.

Despite Tannenberg and other battles that turned on cryptanalysis, the most momentous codebreaking success of World War I involved a diplomatic rather than a military message. The deciphering of that message pulled America into the war and virtually guaranteed the defeat of Germany and her allies.

Throughout the first two years of the conflict, the United States had remained neutral. Although public support seemed to be gradually shifting toward England and France, there existed no consensus on whether America should join the fight, and President Woodrow Wilson won reelection in 1916 largely because he had kept America out of the European war. But a message that originated in Berlin on January 16, 1917, would galvanize American support for joining the fight. The message came from the desk of Germany's foreign minister, Arthur Zimmermann.

In an effort to cut Great Britain's supply lines, the Germans had decided to embark on a policy of unrestricted submarine warfare: they would sink any ship plying the waters around the British Isles, whether it flew the flag of Germany's enemies or of a neutral nation. The decision would carry risks. The sinking of American vessels might turn the United States against Germany. In an effort to deal with that possibility, Zimmermann dispatched a coded cable to Germany's ambassador in Washington, Johann von Bernstorff, directing him in turn to relay the message via telegraph to the German embassy in Mexico City. By arrangement with the United States, German diplomatic cables between Berlin and Washington, D.C., were sent with U.S. State Department traffic because the British had cut all German transmission lines shortly after the start of the war. Unbeknownst to Germany or the United States, however, the British had also tapped American cables. Zimmermann's message was thus intercepted and sent to England's cryptanalytic bureau, Room 40.

Though the message had been transmitted in a new

code that Room 40 had not yet broken, two cryptanalysts managed to produce a partial text by January 17. British authorities immediately recognized that they had been handed a diamond in the rough. The cable seemed to be inviting a third country, perhaps Mexico, to join Germany in an alliance against the United States.

In February, a British agent in Mexico City got a copy of the Zimmermann telegram from a telegraph clerk there. Fortunately for the British, von Bernstorff had relayed the message in a code that Room 40 had broken. The now-readable document directed Germany's imperial minister in Mexico, Heinrich von Eckhardt, to approach Mexico's president with a proposal in the event that the United States entered the war. If Mexico agreed to fight against its neighbor to the north, Germany would see that Texas, New Mexico, and Arizona, which Mexico had lost in previous wars with the United States, would be returned to Mexico. Von Eckhardt was also supposed to suggest that Mexico approach Japan about joining the alliance.

By late February, the British had made the Zimmermann telegram available to the American embassy in

The Text of the Zimmermann Telegram

We intend to begin unrestricted submarine warfare on the first of February. We shall endeavor in spite of this to keep the United States neutral. In the event of this not succeeding, we make Mexico a proposal of alliance on the following basis: Make war together, make peace together, generous financial support, and an understanding on our part that Mexico is to reconquer the lost territory in Texas, New Mexico, and Arizona. The settlement in detail is left to you.

You will inform the President [of Mexico, Venustiano Carranza] of the above most secretly as soon as the outbreak of war with the United States is certain and add the suggestion that he should, on his own initiative, invite Japan to immediate adherence and at the same time mediate between Japan and ourselves.

Please call the President's attention to the fact that the unrestricted employment of our submarines now offers the prospect of compelling England to make peace within a few months. Acknowledge receipt.

Zimmermann

London, which promptly notified President Wilson. On March 1 the decoded telegram was printed in major American newspapers, initiating a stream of anti-German editorials. Public opinion turned decisively against Germany, and on April 6 Congress declared war.

In the area of codes and ciphers, America began the war totally unprepared. Unlike all the other combatants, the United States had no communications intelligence organization. With the sophisticated codebreaking techniques they had evolved, the Germans could have made easy work of existing American military codes. Soon, however, the situation was rectified when a young State Department clerk named Herbert Yardley was commissioned a second lieutenant in the army and charged with setting up a cryptology section attached to Army Intelligence. Yardley learned much from the British, and by the time the war had ended in November 1918, his group, MI8, had created new military codes for the United States and broken several German codes and ciphers.

One of the war's lessons, Yardley believed, was that the United States needed a permanent cryptology organization or it would be at a disadvantage against other world powers. After a bit of lobbying, American officials agreed. In 1919 the American Black Chamber, a 20-person unit that worked for both Army Intelligence and the State Department, was set up under Yardley's direction. The Black Chamber soon proved its worth. It broke Japanese diplomatic codes in advance of the 1921 naval disarmament conference. This alerted American negotiators to secret preconference

Herbert Yardley set up the Black Chamber, the first permanent U.S. cryptographic unit, in 1919. The Black Chamber reported to Army Intelligence and the State Department. Although its successes helped improve America's position as a world power, the Black Chamber was disbanded in 1929.

communications between Japan and Great Britain and revealed the least favorable terms Japan was willing to accept. Those, of course, were the terms the United States negotiated.

Despite its important successes, the Black Chamber ran into trouble only a decade after its establishment. The Hoover administration initially slashed its funding. Then, in October 1929, Secretary of State Henry Stimson decided to pull the plug altogether. "Gentlemen," Stimson said indignantly, "do not read each other's mail."

Fortunately for the United States, Stimson's decision to get rid of the Black Chamber didn't leave America completely in the dark. In 1921, the U.S. Army had established the Signal Intelligence Service (SIS) under the leadership of a brilliant eccentric named William F. Friedman.

Friedman had distinguished himself as a first-rate codebreaker during World War I, solving the German army's principal field code with the help of his wife, Elizabeth, who was also an extraordinary cryptanalyst. After the war, the American Telephone and Telegraph company (AT&T) developed a commercial enciphering device it believed was unbreakable. As a marketing ploy, AT&T challenged the now-well-known Friedman to crack its system. He accepted. A mere four months later, Friedman was reading every message enciphered with the AT&T machine. Recognizing his genius, the U.S. Army hired him and his wife to set up the SIS.

Despite his success with the AT&T machine, Friedman realized that increasingly sophisticated encryption devices were going to revolutionize cryptology. Previously, intuition and an ability to see patterns had been the codebreaker's stock-in-trade. But machine-generated ciphers could be so complex that any patterns would be virtually impossible to discern. Friedman therefore hired the most talented mathematicians he could find for SIS. Mathematical principles would be needed to unravel the secrets of the most complex ciphers.

By the 1930s the army had directed Friedman's SIS to give top priority to reading the communications of Japan, whose expansionist policies in the Pacific augured conflict with the United States. But the dozen or so cryptanalysts who made up the SIS faced a formidable obstacle: Japan had committed itself to developing the most complex cipher machine in history. The Japanese called the result of that commitment Alphabetic Typewriter 97; Friedman code-named the machine PURPLE.

The Japanese had been spurred to action by the publication of a book by Herbert Yardley. In it the former head of the Black Chamber revealed that American codebreakers had read Japan's diplomatic messages throughout the 1920s. Japan was determined not to let that happen again. The first step was to obtain an Enigma machine from its ally, Nazi Germany.

Germany's Enigma, the state-of-the-art in encryption technology, grew from a basic design devised around 1918 by the German electrical engineer Arthur Scherbius. Swiss engineers brought out an improved model, which they called Enigma, in 1923. The Swiss had intended to sell their machines to multinational corporations that needed to protect their communications from competitors. But German authorities, recognizing Enigma's military potential, purchased the patent rights, banned commercial sales, and set engineers to work on further improving the design.

By the mid-1930s the Germans had created an astonishingly secure enciphering machine that was easy to operate and could be made small enough for use in the field. Battery powered, Enigma used electricity to encipher and decipher messages. It consisted of four basic components: a regular typewriter keyboard; a rotor board, which contained multiple, independently spinning rotors, or wheels, on the outer surface of which were each letter of the alphabet; a plug board containing 26 or more sockets; and a backlit light board arranged identically to the typewriter keyboard.

In basic terms, here is how Enigma worked:

- The operator set the machine's initial key settings (the position of each rotor, the internal wiring in each rotor, and the four sockets on the plug board into which were plugged two dual-plug cables) according to predetermined instructions. Initial key settings were changed daily.
- As the operator typed in the first letter of the message, the machine sent an electrical signal to the plug board, where it traveled through the first dual-plug cable, changing the letter.
- From the plug board, the signal traveled to the rotor board. As it passed through each spinning rotor, the letter was changed again. When the signal had reached the final rotor, it was transmitted back through the rotor board, and each rotor again changed the letter.
- From there the signal traveled back to the plug board and went through the second dual-plug cable, thus changing the letter again.
- Finally the signal was sent to the light board, where it illuminated one of the letters. The operator or an assistant wrote down that letter, which became the first letter in the ciphered message.

After the entire message was enciphered in this manner, it was typically then transmitted in Morse code via radio. On the receiving end, an operator typed in the enciphered message on an identical Enigma machine with the same initial key settings, and the machine deciphered it.

Enigma's electrical circuitry made its ciphers virtually random. Because the rotors spun, the same plaintext letter could result in a different ciphered letter each time it appeared in the message. And the

PLAYFAIR CIPHER

Key Word MACARTHUR

A student explains the Playfair cipher to others in his cryptology group. A cipher is different from a code in that the message is altered by systematically substituting characters for the original letters. A code uses a predetermined word or number group to stand for a word in the message.

huge number of possible initial key settings—which were what actually determined how the enciphered message would end up—created a staggering number of possible letter combinations. A three-rotor Enigma, for example, generated about 159 quintillion possibilities (a quintillion is 10^{18}), and Germany eventually developed models of up to 12 rotors. The mind-boggling number of possibilities, the Germans believed, made Enigma unbreakable, even if an enemy managed to capture an Enigma machine.

Nevertheless, after receiving an Enigma machine from Germany, Japan decided to add another level of protection. Its Alphabetic Typewriter 97 enciphered each message and then enciphered the result, raising the possible letter combinations of each keystroke to an incomprehensible number.

By the late 1930s, William Friedman's SIS began seeing intercepted Japanese communications in a cipher that defied solution by any known method. Japan's Alphabetic Typewriter 97 had gone on-line. Friedman correctly surmised that Japan had created a complex new enciphering machine—the machine he called PURPLE. As tensions between the United States and Japan grew, the pressure to crack the PURPLE cipher mounted. But it seemed impregnable. Finally, Friedman decided to abandon traditional decryption techniques in favor of a radical new approach. Instead of attacking the cipher directly, his cryptanalysts would mathematically break down the messages, calculate the possible electrical permutations that could produce those messages, and from that try to infer the machine's structure. Next, they would construct a PURPLE machine of their own, into which they could enter intercepted messages for decryption.

The task was monumental, and months passed with no apparent progress. Finally, however, a few important clues emerged. One diplomatic cable sent in a cipher that SIS had already broken was retransmitted using PURPLE. Linguists also knew that Japanese diplomats tended to use highly formal salutations and closings in their letters, and the Americans were able to look for repeated language patterns at the beginnings and ends of enciphered messages. With these clues, the SIS staff eventually managed to mathematically reconstruct the complex workings of the cipher system. In mid-1940 they began the crucial next step: constructing a PURPLE machine. By the end of the year, the machine had been completed. Remarkably, it worked, immediately decrypting more than 90 percent of the intercepted PURPLE messages. Friedman and his SIS staff had, in the words of espionage authority Ernest Volkman, "achieved the technological equivalent of cloning a human being without ever seeing the twin."

The stunning achievement would yield priceless intelligence, before and after the United States entered World War II. In early 1941, before the Japanese attack on Pearl Harbor, Oshima Hiroshi, Japan's military attaché in Berlin, sent a detailed report to Tokyo about Germany's plans to invade the Soviet Union. After the SIS had decrypted the message, President Roosevelt decided to pass the information on to Winston Churchill, England's prime minister. Churchill, in turn, notified Soviet dictator Josef Stalin. Unfortunately Stalin, who had signed a nonagression pact with Adolf Hitler, believed the information to be a British ploy designed to drag the Soviet Union into the war with Germany. When Germany did invade on June 22, the USSR was caught by surprise and nearly overwhelmed.

Major William F. Friedman was hired by the U.S. Army to set up the Signal Intelligence Service (SIS). During World War II, his group was charged with cracking the Japanese PURPLE cipher.

Though PURPLE decryptions throughout 1941 showed the deterioration of Japan's relationship with the United States and hinted at Japanese plans to strike somewhere in the Pacific, Pearl Harbor was never specifically mentioned. Japan's December 7 attack on the naval base was a surprise. Thereafter, however, intercepted and decrypted messages, both diplomatic and military, gave American commanders key information about Japanese battle plans. They played a major role in the U.S. victory at the Battle of Midway in June 1942, a turning point in the war with Japan. Later, in the war's final months, they indicated that Japan wasn't considering a surrender to avert a U.S. invasion of the Japanese islands. This knowledge may have contributed to President Truman's decision to drop atomic bombs on Hiroshima and Nagasaki.

Although the United States read their most sensitive communications for five years—and gained an incredible advantage during the war—the Japanese never entertained the possibility that Alphabetic Typewriter 97 might be compromised. Their invention, they believed, was simply too ingenious to be defeated. Such complacency in the world of espionage is, history shows, a recipe for disaster.

Japan's Nazi allies, who were similarly overconfident about the invulnerability of their Enigma machine, also paid a heavy price. The success of Britain's ULTRA program, aimed at breaking the Enigma cipher, contributed to many important English victories: the defeat of Germany's numerically superior air force, the Luftwaffe, in the Battle of Britain; the crucial British victory at El Alamein in North Africa; the suppression of German U-boat "wolfpacks" in the North Atlantic; and even the success of the Allies' 1944 D-day invasion at Normandy.

ULTRA, centered at the Government Code and Cipher School at Bletchley Park just outside London, gathered Great Britain's ablest mathematicians, electrical engineers, and linguists for the purpose of breaking Enigma. The British cryptanalysts built on the prewar work of Polish codebreakers, who had constructed machines called *bombes* that simulated the movements of Enigma's rotors. The Poles had themselves received from France documents about Enigma's design and use, which a German cipher clerk had sold to the French in 1931. But Germany's continual upgrading of its Enigma devices—for example, by adding more rotors—had outstripped the Poles' decryption capability.

Bletchley Park's specialists improved the Polish bombes, but, as the Germans had believed, finding the daily initial key settings, without which no messages could be decrypted, remained a formidable problem. In several cases, the British recovered actual Enigma machines and up to a month's worth of naval key settings from sunken or disabled German vessels. In addition, careless German practices—such as choosing obvious initial rotor settings like *ABC*—made the British cryptologists' work much easier. But the real turning point came when a brilliant English mathematician named Alan Turing realized that the bombe's ability to work out Enigma rotor settings was hampered by its lack of a memory. Each time a bombe was cranked up, it essentially began the task from scratch. To rectify this situation, Turing built a large, electromechanical device he dubbed the Bronze Goddess. It rapidly tested possible key settings against the enciphered message using what amounted to a stored memory—all the possible combinations, which Turing had incorporated into a mathematical algorithm. In essence, the Goddess operated under the same principles as the modern computer.

In the decades following the war, the work of Alan Turing contributed to the development of computers. This led to a quantum leap in the complexity of encryption systems. But what can be generated with computers can in theory be solved with computers. So, while the tools of the trade have changed somewhat, cryptanalysts for the world's major nations continue to toil at breaking other nations' cipher systems, and spies willing to steal and sell encryption secrets remain precious assets. And they always will.

Germany considered its Enigma cipher machine unbreakable. Great Britain's best mathematicians, working together in the ULTRA program, proved the Nazis wrong. The Allies used information from decrypted German messages to win important battles during World War II.

U.S. Department of Justice
United States Marshals Service

WANTED
BY U.S. MARSHALS

NOTICE TO ARRESTING AGENCY: BEFORE ARREST, VALIDATE WARRANT THROUGH NATIONAL CRIME INFORMATION CENTER (NCIC).

UNITED STATES MARSHALS SERVICE NCIC ENTRY NUMBER: (NIC/___W224966144___).

NAME: CHRISTOPHER JOHN BOYCE

AKA(S):

DESCRIPTION:

SEX:	MALE
RACE:	WHITE
PLACE OF BIRTH:	SANTA MONICA, CALIFORNIA
DATE(S) OF BIRTH:	FEBRUARY 16, 1953
HEIGHT:	5'9"
WEIGHT:	160
EYES:	BLUE
HAIR:	BROWN
SKINTONE:	
SCARS, MARKS, TATOOS:	
SOCIAL SECURITY NUMBER(S):	566-94-9235
NCIC FINGERPRINT CLASSIFICATION:	16 04 TT 10 03 16 54 TT 04 05

ADDRESS AND LOCALE:

WANTED FOR:	ESCAPE T 18 USC 751
WARRANT ISSUED:	LOS ANGELES, CALIFORNIA
WARRANT NUMBER:	19347-148
DATE WARRANT ISSUED:	JANUARY 21, 1980

MISCELLANEOUS INFORMATION:

VEHICLE/TAG INFORMATION: BOYCE was convicted of ESPIONAGE in LOS ANGELES, California on June 20, 1977. Sentenced to 40 years. Escaped from FCI Lompoc, Ca. 1-21-80.

IF ARRESTED OR WHEREABOUTS KNOWN, NOTIFY THE LOCAL UNITED STATES MARSHALS OFFICE, (TELEPHONE:_____).

IF NO ANSWER, CALL UNITED STATES MARSHALS SERVICE COMMUNICATIONS CENTER IN WASHINGTON, D.C. TELEPHONE _703-285-1100_____: NLETS ACCESS CODE IS DCUSM0000.

(24 Hour telephone contact)

Eyes in the
Skies, Ears
on the Ground

On the first Tuesday of any month, a particularly observant resident of Mexico City glancing out the window of a bus or car might have noticed something unusual along the Avenida Insurgentes, the city's major north-south thoroughfare. Decorating a row of lampposts would be a series of white X's, each a meter from the ground and fashioned with surgical tape. By Wednesday the X's, like a mirage in the desert, would have vanished.

In the bustling capital of Mexico, home to more than seven million souls, only four people understood the significance of the cryptic markings, which began appearing in 1975. The X's signaled three Russian intelligence operatives—Vasily Ivanovich Okana; his driver, Karpov; and General Mikhail Vasilyevich Muzankov—that their young American friend had arrived bearing gifts.

The American was Andrew Daulton Lee, a small-time drug dealer from California whose illegal traffic in

Christopher Boyce (a.k.a. "the Falcon") briefly escaped from prison after his conviction for selling secrets about U.S. spy satellite technology to the Soviet Union. Methods of collecting information about another country's activities have changed significantly over the past 50 years.

cocaine would in time earn him the nickname "the Snowman." But the gifts Lee brought were not illicit drugs. They were documents Lee's childhood friend Christopher Boyce had obtained from his employer. Boyce, whose lifelong passion for training birds of prey formed the basis of his nickname—"the Falcon"—worked for the defense contractor TRW. Ironically, most of the documents he gave Lee to sell to the Russians concerned birds of another sort: spy satellites. Such satellites are a prime source of what is known in intelligence circles as technical espionage, or technical collection. In other words, they collect information without relying on human sources.

Before the 20th century, technical collection was impossible. But in the modern world, the ever-accelerating pace of scientific and technological innovation has given birth to an astounding array of instruments of technical collection. Some observers have even predicted that technology will eliminate the need for human spies. Most experts disagree, however. Instances abound of cases in which an intelligence agency had all the necessary information but no well-placed human source to put it into perspective; there is no substitute for human insight. Nevertheless, technical collection remains a vital component of espionage.

Among the most important instruments of technical collection are spy satellites. From their orbits hundreds of miles above the earth, these satellites can intercept, and relay to ground stations, the radio or microwave communications of foreign governments or militaries. They can also produce, and instantly transmit to an intelligence center, images of what is happening on the ground—on clear or cloudy days and in a level of detail that enables analysts to see objects less than a foot across.

Since ancient times, humankind has dreamed of flying, of rising off the ground and seeing the world from a bird's-eye view. Even before the Wright brothers achieved the technological breakthrough of powered flight in December 1903, military commanders had taken the first tentative steps toward using a bird's-eye view for espionage. During the American Civil War, Union forces besieging Richmond, Virginia, in 1862 first used hot-air balloons to spy on Confederate defenses. This early aerial espionage had limited success. Balloons cannot be steered but go where the wind carries them, so the Union balloons had to be tethered to the ground, restricting observers' views and presenting an irresistible target for Confederate marksmen.

By World War I, however, airplanes and aerial photography had been in use for a number of years. At the outbreak of hostilities, Great Britain moved quickly to establish squadrons devoted to aerial photography and on-ground units of photo interpreters to analyze the pictures produced. Three years into the war, this system was producing daily maps of the entire western front, giving Allied commanders a timely view of enemy positions and early warning of large troop movements.

Though the efficacy of aerial espionage had been established, nations were reluctant to spy on one another from above after the war ended. This reluctance probably reflected a sense that, with the technology of the era, the risks outweighed the possible benefits during peacetime. As international tensions rose in the 1930s, however, intelligence organizations began to arrange spy flights to monitor the activities and identify possible bombing targets of potential enemies. A German unit, the Experimental Post for High-Altitude Flights, which was later renamed the Squadron for Special Purposes, flew espionage missions over Poland, Czechoslovakia, the Soviet Union, France, and Great Britain throughout the 1930s. Sometimes the pilots flew at altitudes too high to be seen from the ground. Other times, wearing civilian clothes, they flew low over cities in planes disguised with commercial markings. Their cover story was that they were developing commercial airline routes. For their part, Great Britain and France collaborated on an aerial spying effort that targeted Germany after the Nazis had made traditional spying extremely difficult within the Reich's borders. Beginning in the mid-1930s, a Royal Air Force pilot named Sidney Cotton, posing as a businessman with an aeronautical research and sales company, flew over and photographed Germany many times. The camera, hidden in a false fuel tank that Cotton could open in flight using a cockpit switch, took clear pictures to an altitude of 20,000 feet. In July 1939,

Tools of the Trade

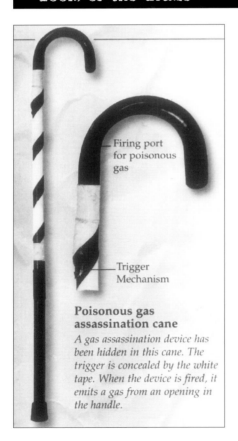

Firing port for poisonous gas

Trigger Mechanism

Poisonous gas assassination cane

A gas assassination device has been hidden in this cane. The trigger is concealed by the white tape. When the device is fired, it emits a gas from an opening in the handle.

The world's best-known spy may be a British agent by the name of James Bond. Of course, he is purely fictional. In numerous motion pictures, beginning with 1962's *Dr. No,* Bond has managed to foil a host of international conspiracies and single-handedly save the free world—all without mussing his elegantly tailored suits. This despite the fact that he makes scant effort to conceal his identity and his job—curious behavior for someone in the espionage business. Bond also romances an army of beautiful women, which no doubt contributes to the enduring popularity of the series, as does his use of an array of the most improbable spy gadgets.

At least one thing about the Bond movies is realistic: the gadgets. The unique needs of spies have spurred some exceedingly creative uses of technology. Tools of the trade include miniature cameras in the shape of all manner of everyday objects, such as matchboxes,

This cane, which fired poison gas, was one of many spy gadgets that were shown to the public during the CIA's 50th anniversary in 1997.

just weeks before the outbreak of World War II, Cotton took his specially outfitted plane to an airshow in Frankfurt, Germany. When the German general Albert Kesselring asked to be taken for a ride in the plane, Cotton complied. Not wanting to miss an opportunity to get photos of the Rhine area over which they flew, the RAF pilot turned over the controls to Kesselring and flipped the switch that activated the camera, explaining that the flashing green light on the cockpit control panel meant that the fuel supply to the engines was normal.

cigarette lighters, and wristwatches. Video cameras that are only slightly larger than postage stamps use advanced optics to film through a cotton shirt or baseball cap, making them easy for the spy to conceal. Secret documents are also easy to conceal with a microdot camera, which produces negatives only a few millimeters square. Inserted under doors, fiberscopes similar to those used in medical procedures enable spies to see into locked rooms, and extremely sensitive night-vision devices help them see in near-total darkness. From outside a building, parabolic microphones can pick up a conversation—or even keyboarding—by reading the invisible vibrations that the sounds produce on window glass. Tiny microphones, called bugs, have been incorporated into every imaginable object, down to the olive in a martini.

To track the contacts of suspected CIA case officers, the Soviets developed an invisible chemical, nitrophenylpentadienal, which came to be known as "spy dust." KGB agents would sprinkle small amounts of the chemical, which is visible only under ultraviolet light, on the steering wheels or door handles of the suspected CIA officers' cars. The dust was easily transferred from one person to another by handshakes or the handling of packages. It could also be sprayed on shoes and used to literally follow a suspect's footsteps.

In the realm of spy weapons, intelligence services have developed many cleverly concealed varieties. A female East German agent was captured with a lipstick container that, when twisted, fired a bullet. Single-shot weapons have also been made to look like pens, pencils, flashlights, and tobacco pipes. The Bulgarian intelligence service used a special umbrella to murder Georgi Markov, a dissident living in London, in 1978. The assassin brushed the tip of the umbrella against Markov's thigh, firing a tiny pellet of poison under the victim's skin. Other assassination devices developed by the KGB included a cane that released deadly gas, and a wallet that did the same.

The United States, also, may have conducted some pre–World War II aerial espionage. Indeed, some intelligence experts believe that the famous American aviator Amelia Earhart—who, along with her navigator, Fred Noonan, disappeared over the Pacific Ocean in 1937 while attempting an around-the-world flight—was actually on a spying mission against strategic Japanese-controlled islands.

Whether or not this is true, the United States, like all the combatants in World War II, made abundant use of aerial espionage during the war. The critical tasks of identifying targets for bombing raids and later assessing the damage inflicted by those raids depended in large part on spies in the air. So did monitoring buildups of men and materiel—an indicator of planned offensives.

In the months before the D-day invasion of Normandy, the Allies decided to try to fool German aerial espionage. In the East Sussex countryside of England, across the English channel from France's Pas de Calais, the Allies constructed an army—thousands and thousands of tents, tanks, artillery pieces, and aircraft—all made of rubber. When German spy planes spotted and photographed the phony installation, Nazi intelligence officers saw a convincing piece of evidence that the coming Allied invasion would be in Calais, not Normandy, and Germany concentrated its defenses there.

Large-scale aerial espionage would never again be reserved for wartime. The world's powers, particularly the United States, made it a priority to develop the capability to carry out such espionage all the time. Concern about the Soviets' nuclear and missile programs helped the CIA get funding in 1954 for a new spy plane, the U-2. With a cruising speed of 460 miles per hour and an operational ceiling of 68,000 feet, the U-2 flew too fast and too high to be intercepted by any Soviet plane, and it remained out of range of Soviet antiaircraft missiles. Outfitted with a state-of-the-art camera that could clearly photograph details as small as one foot, the U-2 flew its first espionage mission over the Soviet Union in 1956. Over the next four years CIA pilots routinely violated Soviet airspace to photograph military bases, missile launchers, and nuclear test sites. The USSR vehemently protested, but the United States denied the incursions. It even denied that the U-2 was a spy plane, saying that its purpose was meteorological research.

On May 1, 1960, CIA pilot Francis Gary Powers took off from a base in northern Pakistan. His flight was intended to produce information on ballistic missile facilities in the USSR. This would be of use to President Dwight D. Eisenhower, who was scheduled to meet with his Soviet counterpart, Nikita Khrushchev, at a superpower summit in Paris. Over the Soviet city of Sverdlovsk, however, the engine of Powers's U-2 flamed out from lack of oxygen. Powers had to glide to a lower altitude to restart the engine, putting him within range of the SA-2, a new Soviet antiaircraft missile. A near-miss explosion of an SA-2 was enough to bring the U-2 down.

The U-2 had a self-destruct mechanism, but Powers had been unable to deploy it; like other U-2 pilots, he carried poison with which to take his own life, but he parachuted successfully and was quickly captured on the ground. Thus, unbeknownst to the CIA and President Eisenhower, the Soviets had the wreckage of a spy plane and a live pilot. Eisenhower denied the U-2

When Francis Gary Powers's U-2 spy plane crashed in the Soviet Union, the pilot and the wreckage of his downed plane were publicly exhibited by Soviet premier Nikita Khrushchev. The incident was a great embarrassment to the United States and to President Dwight D. Eisenhower, who previously had denied spy-plane overflights of the USSR.

incident, but when Khrushchev produced Powers and the downed plane, the president was forced to publicly admit his lie. The espionage disaster embarrassed the United States and its president, produced a worldwide propaganda coup for the Soviets, and effectively ended CIA overflights of the USSR.

But by that time the CIA was almost ready to take

The Trouble with Espionage Trials

Under U.S. law, espionage is punishable by death, but that penalty is almost never handed out. One reason is that defendants frequently have something to bargain with: without the spy's cooperation, investigators may have an extremely difficult time achieving their number one priority—figuring out the extent of the damage. And the government is almost always willing to plea-bargain in an espionage case because of the risk that intelligence secrets will be exposed during a trial. The case of Christopher Boyce, who along with his friend Andrew Daulton Lee passed information about spy satellites to the Soviets, is illustrative.

The two young men were caught in 1977 after a Mexican policeman spotted Lee throwing a note through the fence around the Soviet embassy in Mexico City. When searched, Lee was found to have a roll of microfilm containing photos of documents about Pyramider, a proposed communications system for CIA agents in the field that had never been implemented. Boyce had taken the documents from his employer, the defense contractor TRW. When arrested by the FBI, Boyce confessed that he had passed thousands of classified documents to the Soviets. He was indicted on eight counts of conspiracy and espionage. The case against him appeared strong, and if Boyce was convicted, he could have faced the death penalty.

Nevertheless, when Boyce refused to accept a plea-bargain agreement that would have sent him to prison for 30 years, many in the U.S. government, particularly at the CIA, urged that the case be dropped. They knew that Boyce and Lee had given the Soviets information about Rhyolite, Argus, and KH-11—American spy satellites—and they worried that this fact would come out in court. The United States had never publicly admitted that it had spy satellites. Plus, at TRW Boyce had access to CIA communications traffic. Among the embarrassing secrets he might know were the details of CIA operations against Australia, which the agency had undertaken to safeguard its listening post in Alice Springs. Eventually, though, the government decided to go ahead with the prosecution. It would try to make the case using only small excerpts of Pyramider documents as examples of the many classified items Boyce had stolen.

On April 12, 1977, Christopher Boyce's espionage trial opened in the United States District Court for the Central District of California. Judge Robert J. Kelleher presided. The prosecution introduced a quantum leap in technical collection that would eventually make the U-2 obsolete. In August 1961, just three months after Francis Gary Powers was shot down, the United States launched Discoverer 14, the world's first operational spy satellite. Discoverer passed over and photographed almost the entire Soviet Union.

The first generation of spy satellites had some

Boyce's confession, linked him through physical evidence to the material Andrew Daulton Lee had passed to the Soviets in Mexico City, and finally brought in a CIA expert who testified that even though Pyramider had never become operational, the documents could have proved valuable to the Soviets.

Defense experts attempted to refute the notion that the Soviets could have learned anything useful from Pyramider. Then, on April 26, Boyce took the stand. Gradually, it became clear that the defense strategy was to cast Boyce as a conscientious young man troubled by the actions of his government. He testified that during a party he and Lee had talked about abuses they attributed to the CIA: the assassination of President Kennedy, the overthrow of Chile's elected president. Suddenly, Boyce was testifying about a subject the prosecution desperately wanted to avoid: "I said [to Lee], 'If you think that's bad, you should hear what the Central Intelligence Agency is doing to the Australians.' And he asked me what, and I told him that—"

Before Boyce could give any details, the prosecutor managed to shout an objection, which Judge Kelleher sustained. Later in Boyce's testimony, however, the prosecutor wasn't quick enough to cut off the witness. Again talking about a conversation with Lee, Boyce said, "And I informed him that part of my daily duties [at TRW] . . . I worked in a communication room . . . part of my daily duties were to continue a deception against the Australians."

Still later, Boyce revealed that the CIA had worked to suppress strikes by Australian labor unions. Newspapers seized upon these embarrassing revelations.

But the defense strategy of portraying Boyce as a disillusioned idealist didn't work. Under a withering cross-examination, the prosecutor got Boyce to admit that he had accepted $15,000 from the Soviets for the classified information he provided. The jury took less than four hours to return guilty verdicts on all eight counts. Judge Kelleher eventually sentenced Christopher Boyce to 40 years in prison.

The government had won a victory in court, but it had proved costly. The United States was forced to acknowledge for the first time that it operated spy satellites. Worse, the revelations about CIA operations in Australia were a public relations disaster.

Today, spy missiles are used by ground troops to gather information about the forces aligned against them. This missile was launched by German NATO soldiers to photograph Serb activities in Kosovo during early 1999.

distinct shortcomings. The photos weren't nearly as clear as those produced by spy planes. The film was ejected from the satellite in a cannister, which then had to be recovered by plane and taken to a developing station. This whole process could take days, and in the event of a crisis, the information would be virtually worthless by the time it reached intelligence analysts. And the useful lifespan of the early satellites was only a few days.

But the technology improved dramatically over a relatively short period. By the mid-1970s, the KH-11 and Rhyolite satellites—whose secrets Christopher Boyce and Andrew Lee passed to the Soviets in Mexico City between 1975 and 1976—were marvels of technical espionage. The KH-11, an imaging satellite, stayed in a permanent orbit around 200 miles above the earth. Using digital technology instead of film, the KH-11 beamed real-time images back to ground stations with astounding clarity: objects only six inches across could be seen. Rhyolite used a huge antenna dish to pick up and relay back to ground stations radio transmissions from the USSR or the People's Republic of China at distances exceeding 20,000 miles.

In the two decades since Boyce and Lee's arrest and conviction for espionage, major advances in the technology of spy satellites have occurred. The radar imaging capability of the Lacrosse satellite, which went on-line around 1988, enables it to penetrate cloud cover. Infrared imaging, introduced a year or two later, allows pictures to be obtained at night.

In addition to space-based satellites, technical espionage is carried out on the ground—and even underground and underwater. As with satellite technology, the United States apparently leads in these areas. American listening posts in strategic locations throughout the world capture signals from missile tests, radar emissions (in some cases after they have bounced off the moon), radio transmissions, and cellular phone conversations. Software automatically sifts through the thousands of intercepted conversations for key words or phrases that interest analysts at a given time (for example, the location of a recent terrorist attack).

Conversations or signals that are carried by phone lines or cables do not emit signals into the atmosphere and thus cannot be picked up by listening posts. To intercept them the lines must be physically tapped, which can be a difficult, risky procedure. One of the CIA's most fabled efforts at this occurred in East Berlin.

After World War II, Berlin was divided into French, British, American, and Soviet sectors. With cold war enemies in close proximity to one another, the city became a hotbed of espionage. In 1954 the CIA decided to dig a tunnel that would begin in the American sector under a supposed radar installation and extend some 1,500 feet eastward. The tunnel would run under the fence marking the border with the Soviet

The tunnel that the CIA used to tap the phone lines of the Soviet army headquarters in East Berlin still exists. It was reopened in 1987. The United States and its allies collected important intelligence through the 1,500-foot tunnel for about a year, until it was discovered.

sector and then cross a cemetery, finally culminating beneath a road under which lay the telephone lines used by Soviet headquarters in East Berlin to communicate with Moscow. In a pressurized room sealed off by a submarine-style door—precautions designed to muffle sound—technicians from England's MI6 would tap the Soviet lines. Somehow the Allies managed to avoid detection and complete this ambitious project right under the feet of their adversary. While the tunnel was operational, the Americans and British reaped a bountiful harvest of military intelligence. Within a year, however, the tunnel was closed after East German repairmen seemingly stumbled upon it, though it is now believed that a British spy, George Blake, actually tipped off his Soviet patrons.

More recently, the United States pulled off a similar feat of cable-tapping against the Soviets, though in this case the cable was not underground, but underwater. The program, code-named IVY BELLS, was run in the late 1970s by the National Security Agency (NSA), the supersecret organization that is responsible for intercepting and decoding foreign communications traffic and for protecting U.S. codes and ciphers. A combined NSA–U.S. Navy team traveled by submarine into the Sea of Okhotsk, off the eastern coast of the Soviet Union by the Kamchatka Peninsula, and placed a small, podlike device on a Soviet undersea cable. The device, an improved tap, did not need to physically come into contact with the cable wires but tapped them electronically. It was designed to fall off if the Soviets brought up the cable for repairs or inspection. A tape within the pod recorded all communications traffic over a period of four to six weeks, and twice a year a submarine had to return to the Sea of Okhotsk to retrieve the old pod and replace it with a new one.

Because the Soviets had no reason to suspect the cable wasn't secure, they didn't use their best encryption—and sometimes communicated completely in the open—making the work of NSA analysts easy. In 1981, however, a former NSA employee named Ronald Pelton became a walk-in spy for the Soviets. Among the technical espionage operations he compromised in return for $35,000 was IVY BELLS. The episode was a reminder that while technical collection is a vital component of intelligence gathering, human sources—spies—are indispensable.

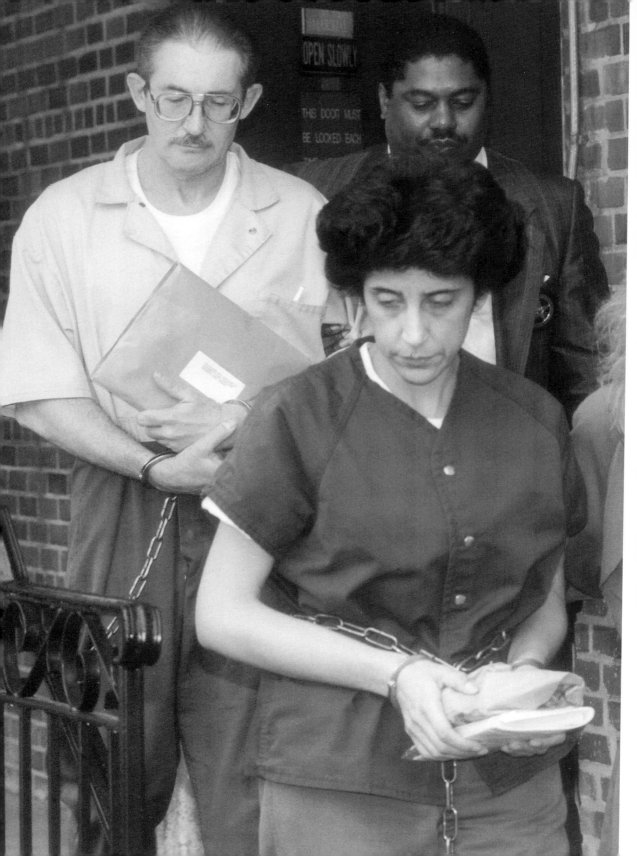

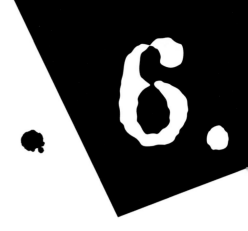

"A WILDERNESS OF MIRRORS"

Aldrich Ames had been the Soviet Union's most indispensable spy for more than a year before the CIA decided it might have a mole on its hands. Initial reviews of the dozen or so cases Ames had compromised in May 1985 pointed to possibilities other than a traitor within the agency's Langley headquarters. Perhaps the KGB had broken a CIA communications code. Perhaps, since all the agents had been arrested after returning to the Soviet Union, there was a leak in the Moscow station. Perhaps the former CIA agent and defector Edward Lee Howard was responsible for many or most of the failures. It was even conceivable that the compromised cases were unrelated. After all, in the high-risk world of espionage, operations were always being discovered and agents rolled up; maybe this situation was no more than a mere coincidence of timing.

While these explanations were not completely unreasonable, CIA detractors point to other, less excusable reasons for the agency's failure to immediately initiate a search for a traitor within its ranks, which is commonly called a "mole hunt." One possibility cited is a sort of institutional hubris—an unwillingness on the part of senior officers to seriously entertain the notion that their organization *could* be penetrated by a mole. Another possibility is that the agency didn't want to relive a terrible nightmare from its past. In that nightmare, the man who played the role of chief tormentor was James Jesus Angleton, head of counterintelligence at the CIA.

Counterintelligence is an extremely important function in any intelligence agency. Nevertheless, as the espionage writer David Wise points out, defining the term precisely can be difficult. Broadly, counterintelligence embraces any effort by an intelligence agency to undermine the effectiveness or thwart the activities of a hostile foreign agency. Obviously, a large part of this involves detecting and neutralizing foreign intelligence operations, arresting spies, and protecting secret information. But counterintelligence is also about uncovering foreign deceptions—and about using deception against enemies, inducing them to chase phantoms or believe disinformation. Counterintelligence also means preventing the worst possible scenario, penetration of one's agency by a mole—and if that fails, ferreting out the mole. It was Angleton's obsession with this final task that earned him the starring role in the CIA's nightmare.

The whole affair started in 1961, when Anatoly Mikhailovich Golitsin, a major in the KGB, defected and was granted asylum in the United States. Golitsin dropped a few bombshells on his debriefers, not the least of which was his assertion that the KGB had a mole inside the CIA.

Obviously, what Golitsin was saying was of keen interest to senior officials and analysts at the CIA, but perhaps none more than Angleton, for if there were a mole it would be up to him, as chief of the CIA's Counterintelligence Staff, to find the traitor. The first step in a case like this was to assess the defector's credibility. There were three possibilities:

1. Golitsin was a genuine defector, and his information was correct.
2. He was not a genuine defector, but rather had been sent by the KGB to achieve some unknown goal—perhaps to spread disinformation or to deflect attention from another Soviet agent or operation.
3. He was a genuine defector, but his information was incorrect.

In time, most people at the CIA inclined toward the third possibility. Maybe that was because Golitsin fingered Israeli prime minister Golda Meir and British Labor Party leader Harold Wilson as Soviet agents. Maybe it was because he claimed the intelligence services of France, Great Britain, Canada, and Norway had all been penetrated as well. Maybe the opinions of a psychiatrist and a clinical psychologist who had independently examined Golitsin seemed hard to ignore. They both diagnosed him as paranoid.

James Jesus Angleton didn't put much stock in the arguments of the doubters. Counterintelligence, he once remarked, is "a wilderness of mirrors," a place where reflections are reflected in still other reflections. Few people could find the truth in this wilderness. Angleton believed himself to be one of those few, and he saw the cunning hand of the KGB where others were bedazzled by the reflections. He simply knew Golitsin was the genuine article.

Angleton's task was to find the mole the KGB defector described: a man who had a Slavic background, who had a last name beginning with the letter K and maybe ending with -sky, and who had been stationed in Germany. His KGB code name was

SASHA. The clues appeared more substantial than they actually were. During this stage of the cold war, Germany was the front line in the espionage battle against the USSR, and many people in the CIA's Soviet division had a Slavic background. Many had Russian parents. Fluency in Russian, after all, was a big asset on the job.

Suspicion fell upon a number of CIA employees who seemed to fit Golitsin's description. Careers were ruined.

By the summer of 1963, with no mole yet found, Angleton expanded the search, showing Golitsin CIA files so that he could point out clues and possible suspects. Golitsin obliged, and the mole hunt consumed more careers. No one was above suspicion; Angleton's job, as he saw it, was to be suspicious. A rueful joke circulated in the halls of CIA headquarters: Angleton suspects himself of being a mole.

By the time Angleton was finally fired in 1974 by CIA director William Colby, virtually everyone who had been in the Soviet division when the mole hunt began had been forced out or had resigned in disgust. In addition, all potential Soviet defectors after Golitsin had been rejected because Angleton suspected them of being KGB plants to throw him off the trail of the mole. "From the mid-1960s on," author David Wise wrote in *Molehunt*, "Soviet operations came to a halt."

Had there ever been a mole? No one can say for sure. Interestingly, a later report by an investigator named Ed Petty concluded that Angleton was the mole. According to Petty, the KGB had sent Golitsin to stir up suspicion at Langley, thus enabling Angleton, as head of the Counterintelligence Staff, to gain access to areas in the CIA that would normally be closed to him. Many CIA analysts dispute Petty's theory, but at least one thing seems certain: counterintelligence *is* a wilderness of mirrors.

When Aldrich Ames became a Soviet mole in 1985,

just 11 years had passed since the end of Angleton's decade-long inquisition. No one at Langley wanted a repeat performance. Yet when nearly all the CIA's best Soviet spies were eliminated, unanswered questions lingered in the air. Finally, in October 1986, with up to 45 Soviet operations now compromised, upper-level officials at Langley decided that the matter needed more thorough investigation. A four-person task force was organized.

Around the same time, the FBI started its own task force to investigate why two agents the bureau shared with the CIA, Valery Martynov and Sergei Motorin, had been recalled from the Soviets' Washington embassy and executed. The FBI had no idea—nor would it know for more than two years—that many

As head of the CIA's counterintelligence department, James Jesus Angleton led a lengthy search for spies inside the organization, called a mole hunt. Angleton's suspicion, based on information from a Soviet defector, ended the careers of many innocent CIA agents and seriously disrupted U.S. espionage activities against the Soviet Union.

other agents had been lost. The CIA withheld this information, even after the respective task forces began meeting informally to discuss leads in the Martynov/Motorin case.

This lack of openness hindered the investigation, but in this regard the Ames case wasn't unique. Mutual suspicion had long plagued the FBI-CIA relationship, in part because of each organization's desire to protect its "turf."

In the United States, intelligence duties are divided among several organizations. When the CIA was created in 1947, some officials worried about the potential effects of a permanent, centralized intelligence organization on Americans' individual rights and liberties. For this reason, the CIA's powers were limited. The agency was charged with conducting foreign intelligence gathering and counterintelligence abroad, but it could not make arrests and was forbidden by law to spy on U.S. citizens. Counterintelligence inside America's borders became the responsibility of the FBI, which was also supposed to conduct most intelligence operations using foreigners within the United States. Unfortunately, the CIA and FBI came to view each other as rivals, and when cooperation was most needed—as in the Ames case—it was often absent.

In late 1986, as the CIA and FBI began their investigations, the man they were actually searching for was no longer in the United States. Aldrich Ames had been transferred to Rome, where he had assumed the position of Soviet branch chief of the CIA station there. While no longer at Langley, as the Soviets would have preferred, Ames still had access to sensitive information. In Rome he passed so many documents that his case officer once sheepishly confessed that the KGB couldn't keep up with the tidal wave of information.

In the summer of 1989, Ames moved back to the United States. By this time he had huge sums of money stashed away in bank accounts all over the world. He

In 1986 the CIA and FBI both started looking for the U.S. spy who was passing secrets to the USSR. However, the two agencies did not always work together and share information. It wasn't until the agencies agreed to cooperate more fully, in 1991, that they were able to identify Aldrich Ames as the spy.

and his wife, Rosario, enjoyed an ostentatious lifestyle. A CIA colleague who knew that Ames had access to compromised cases reported that he seemed to be living beyond his means. The previous year, Ames's name had appeared on a list of 200 possible moles identified by the CIA task force. With the new tip, the task force assigned an investigator to check the Ameses' finances. What he found and reported was extremely suspicious. Unfortunately, however, the investigator was reassigned before he had a chance to follow up.

FBI *agents remove a computer printer from Aldrich Ames's home after his arrest for espionage. One of the key pieces of evidence against Ames was a printer ribbon that contained two important documents. FBI agents had found the ribbon by going through Ames's garbage while the high-ranking CIA agent was under surveillance.*

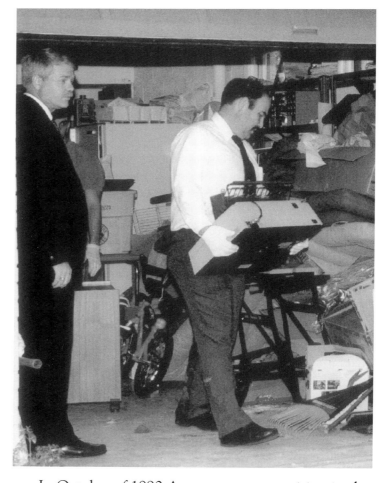

In October of 1990 Ames got a new position in the CIA's Counterintelligence Center (CIC), which had been created two years earlier to upgrade the agency's counterintelligence capability. The CIC had absorbed the special task force established in 1986, so Ames was now assigned to the very department that was investigating him! Although he never had contact with the mole-hunt group, Ames did have access to information of incredible value to the Soviets—namely, the CIA's double-agent operations. Double agents are agents who volunteer for or are recruited by an intelligence service while actually working for a rival service. The service that controls a double agent can use him or her to feed the enemy disinformation, and, from the kinds of things the foreign service asks the double agent to find out, it can deduce what the foreign service does and does not know. When Ames divulged CIA double-agent operations, it enabled the KGB to pass disinformation back to the CIA.

In April 1991, following an agreement between the CIA and the FBI to cooperate more fully in cases of possible intelligence penetrations, the bureau's and the agency's special mole-hunt task forces formally combined. As a result, the investigation, which had stalled in recent months, gathered momentum. By autumn, the joint mole-hunt unit had compiled a list of the top 29 suspects. Ames headed the list, but he had recently passed a lie-detector test, and the other 28 suspects needed to be checked out as well.

Though there is no indication the KGB knew the noose was slowly closing around its best asset, various deceptions the Soviets used to protect Ames did succeed in temporarily diverting the suspicion of the American mole hunters. For example, the KGB forced some of the agents it had arrested as the result of Ames's information to contact their American case officers and inform them that all was well. Other CIA sources who were probably double agents cited poor tradecraft as the cause of some of the compromised operations. Eventually, however, the mole hunters concluded that this was Soviet disinformation.

In late 1991, as the investigation moved forward at Langley, a stunning thing happened half a world away: following a failed coup against Mikhail Gorbachev in August, the Soviet Union collapsed. The cold war was over, and the United States had won. The KGB—the archenemy the CIA had spent 45 years fighting in thousands of ruthless shadow engagements—no longer existed. Still, Aldrich Ames suffered no interruption in his espionage employment; in effect, a different boss was just signing his paychecks. That boss was the SVR, the foreign intelligence service of the newly independent nation of Russia, which could always use a mole in the CIA, even if the prospects of going to war with the United States had declined dramatically. The KGB had meticulously compartmentalized the Ames operation, and his case officers remained the same, so there was little chance he would be exposed by a former KGB agent.

Exposure was nearing anyway, however. A detailed check of Ames's finances revealed that he had made some very large bank deposits in 1985 and 1986, when the CIA's Soviet agents were first being arrested and executed. In late 1992, an investigator cross-checked the dates of those banking transactions with the dates Ames filed reports about his lunch meetings with Sergei Chuvhakin, whom he was supposedly trying to recruit to spy for the United States. Ames had made many deposits, it seemed, immediately after lunches with Chuvakhin.

The mole-hunt unit was now fairly certain that Ames was their man, but it would be necessary to gather enough evidence to win a conviction in court, and that was the FBI's job. In 1993 the CIA turned the case over to the bureau.

In May the FBI opened its investigation, code-named NIGHTMOVER. At work and at home, Ames was shadowed by members of the FBI's Special Surveillance Group (SSG), a unit comprising people of all ages and descriptions who are rigorously trained in the art of blending in with their surroundings. Despite the efforts of about 50 "Gs," as members of the SSG are called, and despite the phone tap the FBI had set up in Ames's home, months passed and the NIGHTMOVER investigators failed to catch the suspect in an incriminating act. Finally, the head of the investigation decided to take a chance. At the risk of tipping Ames off, he ordered that the suspect's garbage can be removed late at night and its contents searched. The gamble paid off: among Ames's trash was a torn note that described an upcoming meeting in Bogotá, Colombia, with his case officer as well as references to dead-drop sites. The evidence allowed the FBI to get a court order for a search of Ames's house. That search, conducted while the Ameses were in Florida for a wedding, yielded conclusive proof that Ames was spying for the Soviets. On the hard drive of his computer agents found detailed records of Ames's espionage activities.

On February 21, 1994, as he was driving to work, Aldrich Ames made a turn and found the road blocked by two cars. Almost immediately, two other cars with flashing lights pulled up behind him. The FBI agents who jumped out quickly slapped handcuffs on Ames and informed him that he was under arrest for espionage. The career of the CIA's deadly mole was finally over.

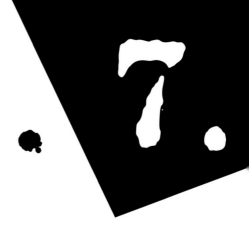

ESPIONAGE AND DEMOCRACY

Yuri Nosenko was as helpless as a shipwrecked sailor clinging to a piece of flotsam in shark-infested seas. For him, however, the end wouldn't come quickly, as the sharks circling the KGB officer wanted more than his flesh. They wanted a confession, and if they had to break him to extract it, that was simply the way the game was played.

The physical and psychological coercion began in the spring of 1964, when Nosenko was whisked away to a house that for the next 18 months would serve as his prison. Guards hauled him up to the attic, where the only furniture was a metal bed bolted to the floor. There was no toilet, only a bucket, and the windows had been sealed over, giving the room an oppressive air.

U.S. district attorney Tom Scott uses a chart to outline a Cuban spy network that was allegedly operating in South Florida. In a democracy, protecting an individual's rights often makes conducting espionage more difficult.

As spring gave way to summer, conditions in the attic became almost unbearable. But the stifling heat wasn't the worst of it. A heavy smoker since childhood, Nosenko was denied cigarettes. Food was scant and foul-tasting. He was allowed to shower and shave only once a week. He had no radio, no books, no magazines—nothing to occupy his mind. His life was a cycle of long, accusatory interrogations—some of which lasted 24 hours without interruption—alternating with periods of boredom, discomfort, and fear.

It seemed to Yuri Nosenko that his predicament couldn't get much worse. He was wrong. Things got decidedly worse when Nosenko's captors transferred him to a windowless, eight-by-eight-foot concrete cell in the middle of a heavily wooded area. During the cold winter months, the light blanket and clothes Nosenko had been given weren't nearly enough to keep him warm in the frigid cell. A TV camera monitored the prisoner 24 hours a day, and when they weren't interrogating him, Nosenko's captors made sure he had nothing to help pass the time. The camera caught him fashioning a chess set from threads, and when that was confiscated he tried to make a calendar, which was also confiscated. Desperate for something—anything—to occupy his mind, Nosenko tried to furtively read the label of his toothpaste under his blanket. The camera caught him doing that as well, and his toothpaste was taken away.

Grueling, hostile interrogations and threats failed to get Nosenko to tell his questioners what they wanted to hear, so they administered drugs. They also gave him a series of lie-detector tests, but these tests were intended less to find out the truth than to intimidate. The examiner screamed that his situation was hopeless and once left Nosenko hooked up to the machine while he took a four-hour "lunch break." Yuri Nosenko suffered through his terrible confinement for four and a half years.

As a member of the KGB, Nosenko knew that this was the way the USSR dealt with traitors and dissenters. He simply hadn't expected this kind of treatment in the United States.

Nosenko had the misfortune of defecting to America after the defection of Anatoly Golitsin, James Jesus Angleton's mole-hunting consultant. Golitsin had labeled his countryman a KGB plant, and Angleton had agreed with this judgment. Angleton was therefore determined to break Nosenko to prove his opinion correct. But others in the CIA wanted to put Nosenko through the wringer for a different reason. When he defected, Nosenko had said that the KGB had no dealings with President John F. Kennedy's presumed assassin, Lee Harvey Oswald, who had lived for a time in the Soviet Union. If Nosenko really was a false defector, that might mean that the Soviets had, in fact, played some role in Kennedy's assassination. So high-level CIA officials wanted to test Nosenko's credibility by whatever means necessary.

Throughout his ordeal, Nosenko stuck by his story, and the CIA finally concluded that he was telling the truth, releasing him in 1968. In an effort to keep the whole sordid affair from becoming public, the CIA paid Nosenko $30,000 for his suffering and hired him as a consultant with back pay. But Nosenko's treatment did leak out in the 1970s, and a congressional inquiry blasted the CIA for its actions. Representative Harold Sawyer of Michigan summed up the mood of his colleagues when he told Richard Helms, director of the CIA during about half of Nosenko's captivity, "You know in most states even treating an animal like this will land you in jail."

Nosenko's torture put a shocking human face on CIA misconduct. But by the mid-1970s, America's espionage establishment was under attack for a host of other offenses, at home and abroad. At home, the CIA had broken the law by spying on American citizens opposed to the war in Vietnam. A massive operation to secretly open and read the mail of private citizens, another felony violation, had also been undertaken. More troubling still, the CIA had conducted mind-control experiments, administering LSD and electroshock treatments to unsuspecting citizens. Some of the human guinea pigs had suffered permanent mental damage; though the records were incomplete, some had probably died.

Abroad, the CIA had been involved in assassination attempts and coups. Working with the American Mafia, CIA agents had tried unsuccessfully to murder Fidel Castro, Cuba's Communist leader. Earlier, in 1954, CIA operatives had played a key role in overthrowing another left-leaning Latin American leader, the Guatemalan president Jacobo Arbenz Guzman. Most galling was the fact that Arbenz had been popularly elected by the Guatemalan people and did not threaten America's security so much as he threatened the profits of an American corporation, United Fruit, whose Guatemalan holdings he wanted to nationalize. Arbenz's ouster was followed by a series of repressive regimes and a decades-long civil war that claimed more than 100,000 Guatemalan lives. Decades of repression and violence also visited the South American nation of Chile following another coup encouraged, if not sponsored, by the CIA in 1972. Like Arbenz, Chile's Salvador Allende had been democratically elected, but he was a Marxist.

The news media treated their readers to stories about these and a host of other excesses committed by the CIA. In addition, two prominent congressional committees—the Church Committee in the Senate and the Pike Committee in the House of Representatives—delved into the CIA's dirty secrets in well-publicized hearings. The outrage was palpable in the halls of Congress and on the streets of the nation.

Americans were right to be outraged, for the CIA had repeatedly broken laws and made a mockery of democratic values. The blanket condemnation of America's espionage establishment obscured a few key points, however. First of all, the CIA hadn't independently decided to assassinate foreign leaders or overthrow foreign governments; authorization for these covert, or secret, operations invariably came from the White House. American presidents used the CIA's covert-operations capability as an instrument of their foreign policy, so if those operations crossed a moral line, the presidents should have shouldered the blame—Eisenhower for the ouster of Arbenz, Kennedy for the Castro assassination plots, Nixon for the coup against Allende.

Chilean president Salvador Allende, shown here reviewing his military troops, was overthrown in a coup encouraged by the CIA. This and other CIA activities—against foreign leaders as well as American citizens—led to increased scrutiny of the agency.

A more subtle point that indignant Americans overlooked has to do with the fundamental contradiction between democracy and espionage. In a dangerous world, a democratic nation needs espionage to detect and counter threats to its security. Yet the requirements of conducting espionage conflict with democratic ideals. Democracy values openness; a basic democratic principle is that citizens should have a say in the decisions of their government, and obviously that requires that they know what those decisions are. In fact, when a democratic government takes action, it does so, in theory at least, in the name of its citizens. But espionage must be conducted in secrecy to be effective. Thus, citizens are in the position of not knowing what their government is doing on their behalf.

As a practical matter, spy operations must not only be kept secret from the public but also be highly compartmented within an intelligence organization, with only a few people having access to all the details. Otherwise, every leak or treason by an individual would compromise entire operations and expose many people to danger. But it is precisely this compartmentation that enabled many of the CIA abuses that came to light in the 1970s to occur in the first place. James Jesus Angleton had a free hand to conduct his outrageous mole hunt, with its accompanying torture of Yuri Nosenko, because only he and a small group of like-minded subordinates had access to all the information—or supposed information—in the case. When everyone is a possible suspect, no one can be trusted with the evidence necessary to independently evaluate the case. Similarly, no independent voice was around to raise ethical or moral objections when a few CIA doctors and agents gave ordinary citizens LSD and other hallucinogenic drugs or administered devastating electroshock treatments. The "research" was considered important because of the fear that the Soviets would use drug- or electroshock-based mind-control techniques against CIA agents. However, in a less compartmented environment that demanded accountability from all employees, it is highly unlikely that involuntary human experimentation would have occurred.

From the intense scrutiny and criticism of the CIA during the 1970s emerged a potential solution to the quandary of how to balance the need for secrecy with the desire for accountability: congressional oversight. The CIA would notify the Senate or House Intelligence Committees when certain operations were undertaken or certain extraordinary conditions existed. In theory, this would preserve the secrecy the CIA needed while creating a check on potentially abusive or ill-advised actions by the agency. Exactly how much detail

Congress needed to know, and when it needed to know, remained issues, however.

Among the first officials to negotiate the minefield imposed by the new rules was Admiral Stansfield Turner, CIA director between 1977 and 1980 under President Jimmy Carter. By all accounts Turner, an intelligence outsider who wanted to reform the CIA's culture of secrecy, tried to comply with the spirit of the oversight laws. His successor, however, proved less amenable.

Unlike Turner, William Casey brought an intelligence background—and a substantial fondness for the venerable ways of espionage—with him when President Ronald Reagan tapped him to be CIA director in 1981. During World War II, Casey had run spies and saboteurs into Nazi-occupied Europe for the Office of Strategic Services, the precursor to the CIA.

Early in his tenure as CIA director, Casey made only a minimal effort to comply with congressional oversight requirements, and from there his effort declined steadily. The Intelligence Oversight Act of 1980 required that the Senate and House Select Committees on Intelligence be "fully and currently informed of all intelligence activities." But Casey's attitude, it seems, was that Congress neither understood nor had the stomach for real-world intelligence and covert operations. Worse, Casey felt, Congress couldn't be trusted with a secret. There was at least some truth in this last view. Often, after a congressional committee had been briefed on a CIA initiative, a committee member or staffer who objected would leak details to the news media. The resulting publicity would force the initiative to be scuttled. In effect, then, a single member of Congress could have veto power over certain operations.

Inevitably, Casey's disdain for congressional oversight figured in a political disaster—a major scandal that rocked the Reagan administration to its foundations

When William J. Casey replaced Stansfield Turner as director of the CIA in 1981, he promised to provide information about the agency's operations to Congress. During his tenure, however, he rarely briefed Congress about important initiatives.

during the president's second term in office. The Iran-contra scandal combined the administration's twin foreign policy obsessions: obtaining the release of American hostages being held in Lebanon by the terrorist group Hezbollah, and supporting the contras, a ragtag army fighting Nicaragua's Communist Sandinista regime.

To Reagan, the CIA-organized and -trained contras were "the moral equivalent of America's Founding Fathers," a group of brave "freedom fighters" battling the tyrannical Sandinista government that ruled their Central American homeland. Many in Congress weren't so sure about this, especially since the contras' military activities seemed largely confined to slipping across the Nicaraguan border from their bases in Honduras, sabotaging infrastructure or attacking civilians, and hustling back across the border before the Sandinista army caught up with them. Nevertheless, Congress initially deferred to the administration, accepting its assurances that the purpose of funding the contras was not to overthrow the Sandinista government but to pressure it into ceasing to arm leftist rebels in the neighboring nation of El Salvador. In 1982 the Boland Amendment, which Reagan signed into law, made this official, explicitly prohibiting the expenditure of funds for the purpose of overthrowing the Sandinistas. The following year Congress authorized $24 million for the contras.

It soon became apparent, however, that the CIA and the administration were being less than candid about the contra operation. Even congressional supporters were outraged with the public disclosure, in April 1984, that the CIA had played a direct role in mining Nicaraguan harbors. That was a violation of international law and a virtual act of war, and the CIA had not fulfilled its requirement to fully inform the congressional oversight committees. In October Congress responded by cutting off funding and banning all direct and indirect support for the contras.

CIA director William Casey, along with a handful of others—most notably a Marine lieutenant colonel named Oliver North, who served as an aide to the president's national security adviser—conceived of ways to skirt the law. Under Casey's tutelage, North set up a private, civilian-run organization to supply weapons to the contras. Foreign governments provided much of the funding. North also devised, and shared with Casey, a scheme to sell arms to Iran, a nation openly hostile toward the United States. Profits from the sales would be diverted to fund the contras, and it was hoped that the Iranians would use their influence with Hezbollah to free the American hostages in Lebanon. Clearly, the Iran-contra scheme violated administration policy of not negotiating with terrorists, and it also flouted the law prohibiting direct or indirect aid to the contras. Plus, it amounted to a rather stunning example of compartmentation: although administration officials knew about the arms sales, the CIA director and a junior officer on the National Security Council staff seem to have kept the diversion of funds from the secretaries of state and defense, and maybe even from the president himself.

In a way America's intelligence environment had come full circle. Abuses stemming from secrecy and compartmentation at the CIA had led to congressional oversight beginning in the mid-1970s. Oversight had functioned for less than a decade before secrecy and compartmentation again won out. The fragility of the oversight arrangement lay in the fact that it required both the intelligence committees and the CIA to act in good faith—the committees by not leaking secrets, the CIA by keeping the committees informed.

The Iran-contra episode, which precipitated the crisis in congressional oversight, cannot be understood outside its cold war context. With a total population less than that of Chicago and an insignificant economy,

Nicaragua might have seemed unlikely to preoccupy the president and the intelligence chief of the world's most powerful nation. But that is what happened, and the explanation, of course, lay in Nicaragua's ties to the Soviet Union. Nicaragua was a small battlefield in a larger struggle between the United States and the USSR, a struggle that had defined both sides' foreign policies since the end of World War II. No direct military confrontation between the two superpowers took place—given their respective nuclear arsenals, such a confrontation could have proved catastrophic—but both nations spent staggering amounts of money preparing for that possibility. Significant sums went toward intelligence and espionage activities.

It's perhaps not too surprising that for the Soviet Union—with its history of totalitarianism and an ideology that exalted the state—the human costs of espionage would not be a great concern. Sadly, however, the strong U.S. tradition of individual rights and protections did not prevent abuses by the American intelligence establishment during the cold war. To a certain extent, perhaps, these abuses—for example, the drug experiments, domestic spying, and assassination attempts—can be explained by the belief that the very survival of the free world was at stake and that the ruthless tactics of the Soviets had to be met with equally ruthless tactics. In other words, in countering the Soviet threat, the end justified the means.

Today, with the collapse of the Soviet Union, the threat no longer exists. Now, no nation can challenge the United States militarily. One might assume, therefore, that the stakes in the espionage game are no longer so high. That's not what the experts say, however. "Yes, we have slain a large dragon," declared James Woolsey, CIA director from February 1993 to January 1995. "But we live now in a jungle filled with a bewildering variety of poisonous snakes. And in many ways, the dragon was easier to keep track of."

The "snakes" Woolsey referred to include terrorist groups, which present special difficulties for intelligence agencies. For a number of reasons, terrorist groups are extremely difficult to penetrate with spies. First of all, to preclude retaliation, terrorists generally take pains to conceal the structure of their organizations and the identities of their members. Often they operate from nations that are hostile to the United States. And typically the groups are small, fanatical, and suspicious of outsiders. Technical espionage is also difficult because terrorists don't operate out of easily identifiable locations such as embassies and don't have large communications infrastructures. Yet small numbers and limited resources don't necessarily equal a small threat. According to federal prosecutors, the handful of Islamic terrorists responsible for the 1993 World Trade

Lieutenant Colonel Oliver North testifies during a hearing on the Iran-contra affair. North was one of a handful of Americans who knew about secret CIA arms sales to Iran and funds that were diverted to support a guerrilla army called the contras, which was fighting to overthrow the Communist government of Nicaragua.

The 1999 revelation that China had conducted an espionage campaign in the United States over a 20-year period highlights the need for counterintelligence to protect national security. The Chinese targeted U.S. nuclear weapons' secrets, such as the design of the W-88 nuclear warhead that is carried on this Trident II missile. Much of the stolen information was taken from America's highest-security nuclear research facilities, indicating the difficulty of maintaining secrets in a society that values the open flow of information.

Center bombing hoped to kill a quarter of a million New Yorkers by toppling the twin towers into the heart of Manhattan. Terrorists could wreak havoc by launching an attack against the computer networks that support America's finance, transportation, or defense systems. And everybody's nightmare scenario, a terrorist attack with a nuclear weapon, isn't far-fetched, according to many experts. The problem is that with the collapse of the Soviet Union, the huge nuclear arsenal the USSR maintained is no longer adequately guarded. Plus, thousands of Russian nuclear scientists are out of work and might be tempted to sell their services. In several documented instances, smugglers have actually gotten nuclear materials out of Russia before being caught.

Of course, terrorists aren't the only ones interested in having a nuclear bomb. The nuclear "club" admitted two new members in 1998 when India and Pakistan successfully tested nuclear devices. More troubling, given the unpredictability of its ruler, Saddam Hussein, is Iraq's nuclear program, which the Gulf War and subsequent United Nations–supervised arms inspections have at least stalled. Whether Saddam and other leaders interested in atomic weapons can be deterred indefinitely remains to be seen.

The fact is that even without the overarching Soviet threat, the world remains fraught with peril for the United States. So as the 21st century begins, the need for espionage remains critical. To believe otherwise would be to ignore experience. In the words of Ernest Volkman, "History has shown that the price of intelligence failure is almost always paid in blood." And to produce good, accurate intelligence without espionage is impossible.

So despite the continual, unresolvable tensions between espionage and the ideals of democracy, the intelligence establishment will go about the secret work of protecting our open society. And while it can be hoped that the worst abuses of cold war espionage won't be repeated, it's inevitable that at the very least a certain moral ambiguity will prevail. "You have to do things that are unscrupulous if you're going to be in the espionage business," former CIA director Stansfield Turner told a TV interviewer in 1998. In the name of a greater good, then, we'll continue to exploit human weaknesses and vices in order to recruit spies. We'll cultivate and reward foreign traitors, even while we condemn our own. As we zealously guard our right to privacy within our own borders, we'll bug the workplaces and homes of foreign officials, tap into and vacuum up the communications of people around the world.

In the no-holds-barred game of espionage, we can be sure that foreign governments are trying to do substantially the same to us.

Further Reading

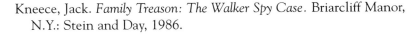

Kneece, Jack. *Family Treason: The Walker Spy Case*. Briarcliff Manor, N.Y.: Stein and Day, 1986.

Lindsey, Robert. *The Falcon and the Snowman*. New York: Simon and Schuster, 1979.

Lloyd, Mark. *The Guinness Book of Espionage*. New York: Da Capo Press, 1994.

Maas, Peter. *Killer Spy: The Inside Story of the FBI's Pursuit and Capture of Aldrich Ames, America's Deadliest Spy*. New York: Warner Books, 1995.

Melton, H. Keith. *The Ultimate Spy Book*. London: Dorling Kindersley Ltd., 1996.

Rhodes, Richard. *Dark Sun: The Making of the Hydrogen Bomb*. New York: Simon and Schuster, 1995.

Richelson, Jeffrey T. *A Century of Spies: Intelligence in the Twentieth Century*. New York: Oxford University Press, 1995.

Schecter, Jerrold L., and Peter S. Deriabin. *The Spy Who Saved the World: How a Soviet Colonel Changed the Course of the Cold War*. New York: Charles Scribner's Sons, 1992.

Sudoplatov, Pavel, and Anatoli Sudoplatov. *Special Tasks*. New York: Little, Brown and Co., 1994.

Turner, Stansfield. *Secrecy and Democracy: The CIA in Transition*. Boston: Houghton Mifflin, 1985.

Volkman, Ernest. *Espionage: The Greatest Spy Operations of the 20th Century*. New York: John Wiley & Sons, 1995.

Wise, David. *Molehunt: The Secret Search for Traitors That Shattered the CIA*. New York: Random House, 1992.

———. *Nightmover: How Aldrich Ames Sold the CIA to the KGB for $4.6 Million*. New York: HarperCollins, 1995.

Woodward, Bob. *Veil: The Secret Wars of the CIA 1981–1987*. New York: Simon and Schuster, 1987.

Index

JOHN ZIFF is a senior editor at Chelsea House. He lives near Philadelphia with his wife, Clare, and children, Jane and Peter.

AUSTIN SARAT is William Nelson Cromwell Professor of Jurisprudence and Political Science at Amherst College, where he also chairs the Department of Law, Jurisprudence and Social Thought. Professor Sarat is the author or editor of 23 books and numerous scholarly articles. Among his books are *Law's Violence, Sitting in Judgment: Sentencing the White Collar Criminal*, and *Justice and Injustice in Law and Legal Theory*. He has received many academic awards and held several prestigious fellowships. He is President of the Law & Society Association and Chair of the Working Group on Law, Culture and the Humanities. In addition, he is a nationally recognized teacher and educator whose teaching has been featured in the *New York Times*, on the *Today* show, and on National Public Radio's *Fresh Air*.

Picture Credits